500

gluten-free dishes

500
gluten-free dishes

the only compendium of gluten-free dishes you'll ever need

Carol Beckerman with Deb Wheaton

APPLE

A Quintet Book

First published in the UK in 2011 by
Apple Press
7 Greenland Street
London NW1 0ND
United Kingdom

www.apple-press.com

ISBN: 978-1-84543-475-5
QTT.FGFD

This book was conceived, designed and produced by
Quintet Publishing Limited
6 Blundell Street
London N7 9BH
United Kingdom

Food Stylist: Jayne Cross
Photographer: John Whittaker
Art Director: Michael Charles
Editorial Director: Donna Gregory
Publisher: Mark Searle

10 9 8 7 6 5 4 3 2 1

Printed in China by 1010 Printing International Ltd.

contents

introduction

It certainly seems as if everyone is talking about 'Going Gluten-Free' these days. Maybe that's why you picked up this book today. Maybe you, or someone close to you, has been recently diagnosed with celiac disease or gluten-sensitivity. The reasons for going gluten-free are many. Besides celiac disease, reasons for considering a gluten-free diet vary from a simple cleanse to a serious and ofttimes controversial weight-loss programme, as well as a treatment for autism and ADHD. Additionally, the newest research identifies a spectrum of gluten-sensitivity, with researchers proposing new nomenclature and classification of gluten-related disorders.

No matter where you find yourself on the spectrum of gluten-intolerance, whether it be celiac, wheat allergy, gluten-intolerance or sensitivity, your treatment will be the same: a gluten-free diet.

This book will demystify the process and get you on your way to enjoying a healthy and satisfying gluten-free lifestyle. The photos that accompany the hundreds of irresistible recipes here will remind you that we eat with our eyes first. In addition to a celiac and gluten-intolerant overview, you will find hints for stocking your pantry and creating a safe cooking space. All of it designed around easy to follow recipes that the whole family will enjoy.

Due to increased awareness, the desire for gluten-free products is growing daily. More gluten-free options are flooding the market as manufacturers step up to address the increasing consumer demand. One trip to the super market will reveal the extent to which manufacturers are appealing to the expanding gluten-free consumer.

There is no need for despair; as you are about to learn, there has never been a better time to be gluten-free!

celiac disease

In 2005, my daughter and I were diagnosed with an incurable disease... And we've been celebrating ever since. Such a bold statement begs an explanation, right? My daughter and I have celiac disease.

what is celiac disease?

It was a London pediatrician, Dr. Samuel Gee, who first put celiac (also called coeliac) on the map in 1888 when he defined the symptoms in children with incredible accuracy and connected it to diet. In the 1950s, gluten was identified as the culprit, but it wasn't until the 1970s that the genetic markers were identified. We now know that celiac disease is a serious genetic autoimmune disease manifested by a complete intolerance to all foods containing gluten. Gluten is the storage protein found in wheat, rye and barley. It's what makes flour sticky and gives bread its unique structure. But for celiacs, even a crumb of gluten-containing food can cause a severe reaction.

what are the symptoms?

Probably the most common and classic symptoms of celiac will be gastrointestinal. However, celiac disease is a multi-system, multi-symptom disorder. Symptoms vary and are not always gastrointestinal. Common symptoms include: bloating, diarrhoea and/or constipation, migraine headaches, brain fog, fatigue, infertility and pregnancy complications, migraine headaches, joint and bone pain, anaemia and slow growth in childhood. There is also a skin manifestation of celiac called dermatitis herpetiformis (DH), characterised by a blistering, intensely itchy skin. DH patients can also have intestinal damage without obvious gastrointestinal symptoms.

If left undiagnosed, related serious diseases associated with celiac include: rheumatoid arthritis, insulin-dependent type I diabetes, osteoporosis, thyroid disease, lupus, liver diseases and certain types of cancer.

Celiac is the #1 genetic autoimmune disease on the planet, as well as being the most under-diagnosed and/or misdiagnosed disease. In fact, 97% of all celiacs don't even know they have a potentially life-threatening disease. The average delay in diagnosis in adults is 9 years.

so why are we celebrating?
Celiac is the only disease in the world completely controlled by diet. Specifically and simply... a gluten-free diet! And that is cause for celebration. *500 Gluten-Free Dishes* will help to demystify the process and get you on your way.

On a gluten-free diet my daughter and I are leading normal, healthy lives. We have our lives back! Adhering to a strict gluten-free diet, it is very unlikely that we will suffer from any of the secondary diseases associated with undiagnosed celiac disease.

what is gluten-sensitivity?
There are also an increasing number of people who experience a celiac-like reaction to gluten without the positive serology or intestinal damage. Those who experience distress after consuming gluten and improvement after removing it from their diet, are now being diagnosed under the umbrella of 'gluten-sensitive.'

The newest research identifies a spectrum of gluten-sensitivity with researchers proposing new nomenclature and classification of gluten-related disorders. If you test negative for celiac but still react after eating gluten, perhaps you fall into this category.

a word about gluten-free oats

Oats are often found on the 'avoid' list for a gluten-free diet. The fact is that oats are naturally gluten-free but often cross-contaminated in the field. Oats are often grown near wheat fields and historically might be part of the crop rotation cycle with other gluten containing grains. Research shows that the majority of celiacs can tolerate certified gluten-free oats and oats are encouraged as part of a balanced gluten-diet as they add protein, fibre and variety. Because of the added protein, GF oat flour is also a great substitute for wheat flour. However, it is true that a segment of the celiac community remains intolerant to even the cleanest, gluten-free oats. My daughter and I unfortunately fell into this population. But new research has given us hope to get oats back into our lives. It seems that most oats have hulls which are very high in a protein called G12. And it seems that it might be this 'avenin peptide' in hulled oats that causes a reaction with GF oats. The fact is that some gluten-free oats test very high in this protein. So even if they are grown in a completely gluten-free environment, they can still be intolerable to some sensitive individuals; celiacs and gluten-intolerants alike. There is a variety called 'Avena nuda L'. This is a naturally 'hull-less' oat which is very low is the avenin peptide that might be the cause or a gluten-like reaction. My daughter and I have found that we can both tolerate it well and oats and oat flour are now a part of our daily GF diet. It you can tolerate oats; the Breakfast Granola on page 45 is a healthy addition to any diet.

but is a gluten-free diet healthy?

Balance is always a vital part of every successful diet and a gluten-free diet is no different in that regard. This is a where a gluten-free diet can really shine, as you won't be tempted by that heavily battered deep fried fish or dough balls. The five daily portions of fruits and vegetables that should be a part of every balanced diet are all gluten-free. All *untreated meat, fish and poultry are naturally gluten-free (*note: some wheat-based fillers are added to processed meats and fish.) Be sure to include starchy carbohydrates such as rice, potatoes, yams and gluten-free grains like quinoa and amaranth. Reduce your total fat intake, especially saturated fat, which is found in animal products such as butter, fatty cuts of meat and full-fat dairy products.

So, what's missing in a gluten-free diet? Experts tell us that a total elimination of gluten from your diet can result in a deficiency of some B Vitamins and fiber, which are abundant in most gluten-containing grains. However, supplementation is simple enough and many gluten-free grains are actually quite high in B vitamins and protein. Among the highest are amaranth, oats, quinoa and teff.

getting started

In preparation for enjoying this book to its fullest potential, we first have to deal with the issue of cross-contamination. The fact is that gluten is a very irritating, sticky pest. Bits of gluten have been accumulating in your kitchen for years and they will be happy to remind you of your fully-glutenised past. So, like any pest, gluten requires a specific extermination plan. In the beginning, this part of the process can be a bit challenging. The good news: you should only have to do this once. Starting with this book, you are taking charge of your future well-being.

Read the labels of your kitchen staples, as gluten is often used in spreads, sauces, flavour enhancers/spices and additives like modified food starch. Also, canned soups and bagged snack foods often contain wheat. But shopping is getting easier every day as many of these foods now proudly proclaim 'gluten-free' on the label. Also, you'll need to check your vitamin supplements, as many contain gluten as filler.

There are also countless lists of safe GF brands on the internet, but when in doubt, call or email the manufacturer. They are happy to hear from us and they want to keep us safe.

shopping hints

- Cooking from scratch is the best way to avoid contamination and increase your comfort level. This book will guide through hundreds of easy-to-follow recipes with a myriad of delightful variations.
- You will quickly realise that there are many more foods that are naturally gluten-free than not.
- Many supermarkets now offer entire sections filled with gluten-free choices.
- Beware of processed foods – if you can't pronounce the ingredients, you should probably consider another choice.

With the proper education and preparation, a gluten-free diet can be easily managed and maintained.

re-stocking the pantry and fridge

It's probably quite apparent that in order to have a gluten-free kitchen, you must remove all gluten. Besides the obvious, there are many gluten-free items in every kitchen that have been inadvertently contaminated. Start with the fridge: condiments like mayonnaise, ketchup and mustard are almost always naturally gluten-free. But once the jar has been double-dipped, spread onto wheat bread and dipped back into the jar, that jar is contaminated... forever. When you replace these items, especially if you have a shared kitchen, consider using squeeze jars and thus eliminate the issue of double-dipping.

de-glutenising your space

- Counter tops: vigorously scrub with a very hot soapy solution.
- Pots and pans: stainless steel is the easiest to de-gluten and can be made safe with one good scour. However, gluten baked on cast iron can be more challenging, as it usually boasts a buildup of years of 'seasoning'. If it's a family heirloom, then scour it with a

stainless steel soap pad, rinse well and bake in a very hot over for about 15 minutes. Otherwise, I hope you will treat yourself to a new cast iron frying pan.

- Pie dishes and cake pans: glass is the easiest to de-gluten. Simply scrub and wash in the dishwasher. Aluminium cake and pie tins and especially Bundt pans, should be replaced.
- Cutting boards: it will probably be necessary to replace your old plastic cutting boards. Notice the little slices and cuts on them? Those signs of wear and tear can trap gluten. Wooden cutting boards, depending on thickness, can often be sanded down to the fresh wood.
- Utensils, rolling pins, measuring cups and spoons: for the same reasons as above, replace both wooden and plastic.
- Appliances: that favourite old toaster or waffle iron is not your friend. Crumbs from your former, gluten-filled life will live there and dust your gluten-free toast forever. A new toaster/waffle iron is in your future.
- After cleaning to de-glutenise your kitchen, toss all of the old sponges.
- Deep fryer: amazingly the gluten molecule will remain active, even in the boiling oil of a deep fryer. Give all elements a very deep scrubbing.

Note: until this point, I have assumed that you will be creating a totally gluten-free kitchen. If you will be cooking in a shared kitchen, a few creative modifications will need to be made.

- In a shared kitchen you will now need to have side by side toasters. Designate your GF toaster by using a laundry marker or tape.
- Designate a separate drawer for GF utensils. Use a marker label the handle. Or better yet, purchase utensils with a different color handle. A color-coding system can be useful throughout your shared kitchen.
- Label or mark the tops of any condiments that are in jars. A simple 'GF Please' works for me.
- Designate separate butter and cheese. Or simply use clean knives for each use.

cooking for the celiac child

Once you have educated yourself, created a safe cooking space and stocked your pantry, in my opinion cooking for your celiac child can be a piece of cake; gluten-free of course!

Every child has their own special food favourites and many of them will be naturally gluten-free. We all know that some kids are just pickier than others. If you've got a picky palate in your household, make it a non-issue as soon as possible by focusing on some of the delicious GF possibilities available in this book. For the younger child, share this cookbook. Gluten-free story time is a great way to engage your child. Allowing your children to make some choices can empower them to take part in their gluten-free diet. Remembering, again that we eat with our eyes first; perusing the beautiful photos in this book is certain to inspire everyone. It's probably not the best idea to tout that spinach and brussel sprouts are gluten-free. Instead, highlight the fact that chocolate and many ice creams are naturally gluten-free. In my experience, school might be the more challenging issue. After diagnosis, a face-to-face parent-teacher conference is essential. Take the guess work out of the issue for your teacher by printing out 'avoid' and 'safe' food lists. We all know that kids hate to feel 'different' and they love to share food. Ultimately, there is no way to sugar-coat it: your child's classmates must understand that they cannot share their biscuits and sandwiches. But imagine the delicious Chocolate Pecan Brownies on page 265 at your child's classroom birthday party. No one will know they are gluten-free. It's very likely that some of your child's classmates will have some sort of food issue or other allergy too. Level the playing field by encouraging your teacher to schedule some time for a classroom 'show and tell' discussion of everyone's 'issues.'

a family affair

The newest research shows that 11% of first-degree family members, such as a parent or a sibling, will also have celiac disease. In fact, in siblings are at an even higher increased risk; at

22%. Look at your family tree; did a grandmother or aunt have an autoimmune disease such as rheumatoid arthritis or osteoporosis? I believe it is essential that we all seek out opportunities to educate our family members and encourage them to be tested.

Whether life-style choice, allergy or serious autoimmune disease (celiac), your success with a gluten-free diet will be dependent upon your desire to embrace the lifestyle. And since it's all about food, there is no doubt that the fabulous recipes in this book will motivate you and diving into the variations noted on each recipe you will quickly discover your own gluten-free style. Finally, a quick internet search will confirm that you don't have to go it alone; there is a world-wide celiac community right at your fingertips. Dozens of support groups, blogs and websites will keep you up-to-date and will confirm that we all have a lot in common. Probably the only thing we love more than sharing the latest recipe for the best gluten-free biscuit is our desire to share the latest research and hints to living your gluten-free lifestyle to its fullest potential.

possible hidden sources of gluten
Many of the following could have gluten. And many now have GF alternatives. Always read the labels and if in doubt, contact the manufacturer.

- baking powder
- barley water or flavoured barley
- flavoured waters
- beer and lager, stout and ale
- bouillon or stock cubes
- brown rice syrup
- cheese spreads
- chips—flour may be used to keep them white
- chocolate
- cold cuts, hot dogs, salami, sausage
- coffee from vending machines
- commercial salad dressings
- corn tortillas
- crisps, potato chips
- dry roasted nuts
- fizzy drinks
- gravy

- ground almonds
- imitation fish (crab)
- malted milk drinks
- matzo
- mustard powder
- packets of grated cheese
- pretzels
- rice mixes
- prescribed tablets
- sauces
- seasoned tortilla chips
- seasoning mixes
- self-basting turkey
- soups
- soy sauce
- vegetable in sauce
- worcestershire sauce

foods that are safe

- fresh meat and fish
- fresh fruit and vegetables
- cornmeal
- corn syrup (such as Karo)
- dairy products (plain/pure)
- dried pulses
- eggs
- fresh herbs and plain spices
- fruit jams and marmalades
- honey
- plain nuts and seeds
- pure oils and fats
- maple syrup and molasses
- rice and wild rice (but not rice mixes)
- rice bran
- GF rice noodles
- GF Tamari Soy Sauce
- soy and plain tofu (note: tofu is often dusted with flour)
- sugar
- tomato paste, tomato puree
- pure vanilla extract
- GF vinegars (note: malt vinegar contains gluten. Some balsamics too)
- whole kernel corn
- yeast, fresh and dried

gluten-free (GF) flour-mixes and pastries

plain flour mix
This is a good basic substitute for the same quantity of standard all-purpose flour. If you use it for baking, add baking powder and other ingredients, as you would in a generic recipe.

170 g (6 oz) white rice flour
100 g (3¹/₂ oz) tapioca flour

85 g (3 oz) potato starch
pinch salt

In a large bowl, whisk all the ingredients together until well blended. Use as required. Store for up to two weeks in an airtight container in a cool, dark place. Do not refrigerate or freeze.

self-raising flour mix
As with all-purpose flour mix above, this is a good basic substitute for self rising flour. As it is self-raising, the baking powder and xantham gum are already in the mix.

170 g (6 oz) white rice flour
100 g (3¹/₂ oz) tapioca flour
85 g (3 oz) potato starch

1 tsp xantham gum
1 tbsp baking powder
pinch salt

In a large bowl, whisk all the ingredients together until well blended. Use as required. Store for up to two weeks in an airtight container in a cool, dark place. Do not refrigerate or freeze.

biscuit flour mix
This is a good basic flour mix to make your favourite biscuit recipes.

170 g (6 oz) white rice flour
110 g (4 oz) potato starch

40 g (1¹/₂ oz) tapioca flour
1 tsp Xantham gum

In a large bowl, whisk all the ingredients together until well-blended. Use as required. Store for up to two weeks in an airtight container in a cool, dark place. Do not refrigerate or freeze.

basic pancake batter

This is a good basic pancake mix, excellent for everyday use. Keep the flours mixed together, stored in an airtight container and just add the liquid when needed.

130 g (4½ oz) white rice flour
100 g (3½ oz) tapioca flour
1 tbsp baking powder
2 tsp sugar
pinch salt

1 egg
300 ml (10 fl. oz) buttermilk or rice milk
2 tbsp butter or dairy-free margarine, melted

In a large bowl, whisk the dry ingredients until well combined. In a medium bowl, whisk together the egg and buttermilk. Make a well in the centre of the dry ingredients and add the egg mixture. Stir lightly until just combined. Pour the melted butter or margarine into the batter, stirring lightly to combine. Spoon onto a hot griddle to make pancakes.

basic pastry crust

Not only is it very tasty, this pastry is made partly using oil rather than all butter, which makes it better for your heart.

85 g (3 oz) white rice flour
60 g (2 oz) cornstarch
30 g (1 oz) buckwheat flour
pinch salt

60 g (2 oz) butter or dairy-free margarine
60 ml (2 fl. oz) sunflower oil
1 tbsp water, plus a little more if needed

Grease a 9-inch (23-cm) loose-bottomed fluted tart pan. Preheat the oven to 200°C (400°F/ Gas mark 6). Make the pastry by sifting the flours, cornstarch and salt together into a large bowl. Add the margarine and cut in with your fingers until it resembles fine breadcrumbs. Add the oil and water and mix to a soft dough. Add more water if necessary. Do not worry about overworking the dough, as this pastry is much more robust than normal shortcrust pastry. Gather the dough into a ball with your hands, flatten it into a circle and place in the pan.

Using your fingers, gently press the dough down to cover the base and go up the sides. Do not press the dough above the edge of the pan. Place a sheet of baking parchment on the pastry, place baking beans on top and bake blind in the oven for 10 minutes. Remove the beans and paper and bake for a further 5 minutes. Remove from the oven. Use as required.

biscuit crust pastry for pie topping

This biscuit crust recipe looks and tastes great. It is easy to roll out and it also works well as a biscuit recipe – just roll thicker and cut into rounds. When the pastry has been rolled out, the normal way of lifting it onto a pie would be to roll it around a rolling pin, but this pastry will crack if you do that. If you roll it to about 0.6-cm ($\frac{1}{4}$-inch) thickness, you should be able to lift it at either end, with your fingers, and place it quickly onto the pie.

130 g ($4\frac{1}{2}$ oz) brown rice flour
170 g (6 oz) potato starch
1 tsp xantham gum
1 tbsp baking powder
1 tsp cream of tartar
1 tsp baking soda
1 tsp sugar

$\frac{1}{2}$ tsp salt
60 g (2 oz) butter or dairy-free margarine
1 large egg
120 ml (4 fl. oz) milk or rice milk
white rice flour for dusting and rolling
a lightly beaten egg, for brushing over the pie

Preheat the oven to 175°C (350°F/Gas mark 4) and have the pie ready that you want to cover with pastry. Dampen the edges of the pie dish with a little water or beaten egg. In a large bowl, whisk the brown rice flour, potato starch, xantham gum, baking powder, cream of tartar, baking soda, sugar and salt together until well blended. Work in the butter or margarine with a pastry cutter or your hands until the mixture resembles fine breadcrumbs. In a small bowl, whisk the egg and milk together. Make a well in the centre of the flour mix and add the egg and milk. Stir with a round-bladed knife until the mixture forms a soft dough. Gather together with your fingers into a ball and turn out onto a work surface dusted with white rice flour. Roll out to little more than a thickness of 0.6 cm ($\frac{1}{4}$ inch) and lift quickly onto the pie. Press down lightly with your fingers to seal to the pie edge, brush with a little beaten egg, make a hole with the tip of a sharp knife in the centre to let the steam escape and bake in the oven for about 25 minutes, until golden brown and crisp.

shortcrust pastry for pie topping

This pastry looks, once cooked, much more authentic than the biscuit crust as a pie topping, but it is much harder to handle. It will crack easily, so to protect it as much as possible it is necessary to roll it out between sheets of clingfilm. This sounds complicated, but in practise, is not. The pastry tastes very good and is well worth the extra effort.

85 g (3 oz) white rice flour, plus extra for
   dusting
85 g (3 oz) fine cornmeal (polenta)
60 g (2 oz) potato starch
30 g (1 oz) tapioca flour
1 tsp xantham gum

pinch salt
140 g (5 oz) butter or dairy-free margarine
1 egg, beaten
1–2 tbsp water

In a large bowl, whisk the rice flour, cornmeal, potato starch, tapioca flour, xantham gum and salt together until well blended. Cut in the butter or margarine with a pastry cutter or your fingers, until the mixture resembles fine breadcrumbs. Stir in the egg and enough water to make a soft dough. Using your fingers, gather the dough into a ball. The dough should not be too wet. Lightly flour the work surface with rice flour and gently knead the pastry a few times. Wrap in clingfilm and chill in the fridge for about 30 minutes before using.

breakfasts & brunches

Weekend breakfasts and brunches are the time to relax with family and friends, enjoying either sweet or savoury treats. Waffles and pancakes are a well-known breakfast staple, but with a little extra thought, the gluten-free variety is as good, if not better.

classic buttermilk pancakes

see variations page 48

These pancakes have buckwheat in them, which, despite the name, has nothing to do with wheat. They are light and fluffy and full of wholesome goodness.

300 g (3¹/₂ oz) white rice flour
50 g (1³/₄ oz) buckwheat flour
2 tsp baking powder
¹/₂ tsp salt
2 tbsp sugar
1 large egg

50 ml (5 fl. oz) buttermilk
1 tsp vanilla extract
2 tbsp (1 oz) butter, plus extra for cooking
icing sugar, maple syrup and butter,
         to serve

Preheat the oven to 135°F (275°F/Gas mark 1). Sift the flours, baking powder and salt into a large bowl, add the sugar and mix together. Make a well in the centre, break in the egg and add the buttermilk and vanilla extract. Stir from the centre with a wooden spoon, slowly incorporating the flour from the sides as you stir. Do not overmix and do not worry about any lumps. In a large frying pan, melt 2 tablespoons butter, tip it into the batter and stir it in lightly. Put the frying pan back on the heat, add a little more butter and swirl it around the base of the tin. When it is nice and hot, but not smoking, spoon about 3 tablespoons of batter into the tin to form a pancake about 13 cm in diameter. If there is room in the frying pan, spoon in another 3 tablespoons more, forming another pancake. The pancakes should make a sizzling sound and begin to bubble. When they look dry at the edges, turn them over. They should have a good brown colour. The second side will cook faster than the first. Place them on a platter, cover and keep in the warm oven while you make the rest. Serve dusted with icing sugar and with butter and maple syrup on the side.

Serves 4

pecan waffles with butterscotch sauce

see variations page 49

These are a delicious breakfast choice. Popular with adults and children alike, these waffles are served with a yummy butterscotch sauce, which is also excellent served over most flavours of ice cream.

for the sauce
115 g (4 oz) butter
3 tbsp light golden syrup
230 g (8 oz) brown sugar
240 ml (8 fl. oz) single cream
2 tbsp lemon juice

for the waffles
140 g (5 oz) white rice flour
30 g (1 oz) tapioca flour
40 g (1½ oz) potato starch

2 tsp baking powder
1 tsp salt
2 tsp sugar
40 g (1½ oz) chopped pecans,
    plus extra for sprinkling
355 ml (12 fl. oz) buttermilk
1 tsp vanilla extract
60 ml (2 fl. oz) canola oil
2 eggs
butter for cooking
icing sugar, to serve

First make the sauce. In a medium saucepan, melt the butter over a gentle heat, add the syrup and sugar and heat until the sugar has dissolved. Add the single cream and lemon juice. Bring to the boil, then simmer gently for 5 minutes, stirring occasionally and set aside to cool. Serve warm or cooled. Preheat the waffle iron. In a large bowl, sift together the flours, potato starch, baking powder and salt. Add the sugar and pecans. In another bowl, beat together the buttermilk, vanilla extract, oil and eggs. Make a well in the centre of the

flour mixture and stir in the milk mixture, beating to form a smooth batter. Once your waffle iron is hot, brush with a little butter and spoon in enough batter to just cover the base. The batter will rise and spread during cooking. Cook until crisp and golden, about 5 minutes.

Keep warm while you make the rest, then serve immediately sprinkled with a little icing sugar and chopped pecans, with the butterscotch sauce on the side.

Serves 6

dutch apple breakfast cake

see variations page 50

Caramelised apples, surrounded by a thick and satisfying type of pancake and topped with a large dollop of crème fraîche, are a wonderful way to start the day.

2 tbsp (1 oz) butter
2 tsp ground cinnamon
3 tbsp sugar
4 tart apples (such as Granny Smith), peeled,
    cored and thinly sliced
35 g (1¼ oz) white rice flour
30 g (1 oz) tapioca flour
40 g (1½ oz) potato starch

2 tsp baking powder
¼ tsp salt
½ tsp xantham gum
3 eggs
180 ml (6 fl. oz) buttermilk
1 tsp vanilla extract
icing sugar and crème fraîche, to serve

Preheat the oven to 200°C (400°F/Gas mark 6). In a large ovenproof frying pan, over a medium heat, melt the butter, add the cinnamon and sugar and mix together. Add the sliced apples to the frying pan, cover and cook for about 15 minutes until softened. Place the frying pan in the oven, uncovered, for 5 minutes. In a large bowl, sift together the flours, potato starch, baking powder and salt. Stir in the xantham gum. In a medium bowl, whisk the eggs, buttermilk and vanilla. Make a well in the centre of the flour and pour in the milk mixture. Stir with a wooden spoon from the centre, slowly incorporating the flour from the sides as you stir.

Remove the tin from the oven and pour in the batter. Return to the oven and bake, uncovered, for about 15 minutes, until risen and golden brown. Serve sprinkled with icing sugar and with a large dollop of crème fraîche.

Serves 4

almond french toast with strawberry topping

see variations page 51

This is the best way of eating French toast, sprinkled with nuts and sautéed in butter until golden brown, but still fluffy inside. Top with strawberries for a wonderful combination of flavours.

450 g (1 lb.) fresh strawberries,
    washed and hulled
110 g (4 oz) sugar
90 ml (3 fl. oz) freshly squeezed orange juice
1 tsp orange zest
1 cherry brioche loaf (page 128),
    made the day before
4 large eggs

150 ml (5 fl. oz) milk
60 g (2 oz) sugar
1 tsp vanilla extract
3 tbsp sliced almonds
2 tbsp (1 oz) butter, for cooking
2 tsp vegetable oil
icing sugar, to serve

First make the strawberry topping. Slice the strawberries 5 mm (1/5 inch) thick and place in a medium bowl. In a medium saucepan, combine sugar with the orange juice and zest and bring to the boil, stirring to dissolve the sugar. Simmer for 2 minutes, then pour over the strawberries. Set aside to cool. Slice the cherry brioche loaf 1 cm (2/5 inch) thick and set aside.

In a shallow bowl, beat the eggs with the milk, sugar and vanilla extract. In a large frying pan, heat half the butter and the vegetable oil, until hot, but not smoking. Dip each slice of brioche into the batter just before cooking and leave just a few moments to soak up the batter, then turn over to soak the other side.

Place slices into the hot butter, sprinkle each with 2 teaspoons sliced almonds and press almonds lightly into the bread with a spatula. Cook for 2 or 3 minutes, until golden brown, then turn over and cook the other side. Remove from the tin and keep warm while you cook the rest, adding the rest of the butter to the tin as necessary. Serve sprinkled with icing sugar and strawberry topping.

Serves 4–5

eggs florentine

see variations page 52

Perfect poached eggs perched on buttered spinach and a crispy buttermilk biscuit and smothered in homemade hollandaise, make a balanced and hearty breakfast.

2 egg yolks
2 tbsp hot water
140 g (5 oz) butter, melted
juice of ½ lemon
salt
pinch cayenne pepper

about 60 g (2 oz) butter,
    for cooking and spreading
85 g (3 oz) fresh spinach leaves
salt and freshly ground black pepper
4 eggs, poached
2 buttermilk biscuits (page 127)

To make the hollandaise, place the egg yolks in a heat-resistant glass bowl over a tin of simmering water. Whisk in 2 tablespoons hot water. Very slowly, add the melted butter, but do not add the milky residue at the bottom of the melted butter. Whisk until all the butter has been incorporated. Whisk in the lemon juice and season with salt and a pinch of cayenne pepper. Set aside.

In a large frying pan, melt a little of the butter and add the spinach. Stir until wilted, then drain and season with salt and pepper. Remove from heat. Meanwhile, prepare poached eggs. Split the buttermilk biscuits in half, spread with butter and divide the spinach between them, leaving a slight indentation on top in which to place the poached eggs, one on each biscuit half. Spoon a quarter of the hollandaise over each egg, then place them underneath a hot grill for 1 minute. Serve immediately.

Serves 2–4

breakfast egg & cheese tortilla wraps

see variations page 53

Quick to make and colourful, these wraps are not only nutritious, but also appetising and appealing for children.

6 corn tortillas
1 tbsp (½ oz) butter
170 g (6 oz) chopped red pepper
60 g (2 oz) chopped green onions
6 large eggs
salt and freshly ground black pepper
140 g (5 oz) shredded Cheddar cheese

Warm the tortillas, either in a dry frying pan or in the microwave, to make them easier to wrap.

In a large frying pan, melt the butter, add the red pepper and sauté for 4 minutes. Add the onions and cook for another minute. In a large bowl, whisk the eggs and season with a little salt and plenty of pepper. Add eggs to the frying pan and stir until starting to set. Add the cheese and continue to stir until the cheese has melted.

Divide between the tortillas and wrap up. Place in the microwave just before serving for 1–2 minutes, until piping hot.

Makes 4–6

potato pancakes with smoked salmon

see variations page 54

These crisp and golden pancakes are traditionally eaten in Eastern and Central Europe, often with soured cream. The addition of smoked salmon makes them a luxurious and indulgent breakfast.

900 g (2 lbs) potatoes
1 small onion
1 egg, beaten
60 ml (2 fl. oz) hot milk

2 tbsp white rice flour
salt and freshly ground black pepper
vegetable oil, for cooking
4–5 slices smoked salmon, to serve

Peel the potatoes and onion and grate them into a large bowl. Mix in the beaten egg, milk, rice flour and plenty of salt and pepper. Mix until you have a thick batter. In a large frying pan, heat a small amount of vegetable oil. When it is hot, but not smoking, spoon in the batter to form pancakes about 18 cm (7 in) diameter. Cook for a few minutes until crisp and golden, then turn them over and cook the other side. Serve with slices of smoked salmon.

Serves 4–5

savoury cheese & onion hotcakes

see variations page 55

For those of us without a sweet tooth, cheese pancakes in the morning fit the bill exactly. With protein, carbs and vegetables, they are an excellent choice for breakfast.

2 tbsp vegetable oil
1 small onion, finely chopped
140 g (5 oz) white rice flour
50 g (1¾ oz) tapioca flour
30 g (1 oz) cornflour
1 tbsp baking powder

½ tsp xantham gum
60 g (2 oz) shredded Cheddar cheese
2 eggs
180 ml (6 fl. oz) milk
salt and freshly ground black pepper

In a large frying pan, heat the vegetable oil until hot, add the onion and cook for 5 minutes, until softened. Remove the frying pan from the heat. Remove the onion from the frying pan with a slotted spoon and set aside to cool slightly.

Sift together the flours, cornflour, baking powder and xantham gum into a large bowl. Add the cheese and the cooled onion and season with salt and pepper. Make a well in the centre, break in the eggs and add the milk. Stir with a wooden spoon from the centre, slowly incorporating the flour mix from the sides as you stir. Do not overmix. You should have a fairly thick batter. Check that you still have about 1 tablespoon of oil in the frying pan and heat it until hot but not smoking. Add spoonfuls of batter to the tin and cook until the hotcakes start to bubble at the edges, then flip them over and cook the other side until golden brown. Keep warm while you make the rest. Serve immediately.

Makes 8

pork breakfast sausages

see variations page 56

Making sausages is much easier than most people think and you can be sure there is
no added gluten. Sausage skins can be purchased from butchers who make their own
sausages or you can dispense with the skin altogether and just roll them into a sausage
shape. You can double the ingredients to make twice the number of sausages, if you can
manage that amount.

2 kg (5 lbs) ground pork
1 tbsp ground white pepper
1 tsp ground ginger
1 tsp ground sage

1 tsp ground mace
2 tbsp salt
230 g (8 oz) GF breadcrumbs or rolled oats
hog casings, rinsed and drained on paper towels

In a large bowl, using your hands, combine all the ingredients (except the casings) together,
evenly distributing the herbs and spices throughout the mixture.

If you have a sausage stuffer on your mixer, thread the hog casings onto it. You will find it
easier to stuff meat into the casings with two people, one to push the meat through and
one to guide the casing off the stuffer, ensuring that there is an even distribution of meat in
the casing. This helps keep the sausages the same size. Keep going until you have used up all
the meat. Twist the sausages into links.

Alternatively, after mixing the sausage meat, roll out on a floured work surface into a
sausage shape and cut into sections about 10–15 cm long (4–6 inches). Refrigerate or freeze
sausages for up to 3 months.

Makes about 2 kg (5 lbs)

sausage biscuits with sun-dried tomato butter

see variations page 57

Everyone loves sausage patties and these are seared over a high heat, making them tasty, filling, with plenty of protein to keep you going until lunch.

70 g (2½ oz) butter, softened
60 g (2 oz) sun-dried tomatoes,
   finely chopped
700 g (1½ lbs) ground pork
1 tsp ground white pepper
½ tsp ground ginger

½ tsp ground sage
½ tsp ground mace
1 tbsp salt
60 g (2 oz) rolled oats or GF breadcrumbs
1 tbsp vegetable oil
8 buttermilk biscuits (page 127)

First make the sun-dried tomato butter. In a medium bowl, beat together the butter and the sun-dried tomatoes until well blended. Set aside to harden in a cool spot, until firm enough to spread. Make the sausage patties. In a large bowl, using your hands, combine the ground pork with the seasonings and oats or breadcrumbs, making sure that the herbs and spices are distributed evenly. Divide the mixture evenly into 8 portions and form into patties. Chill until ready to use.

In a large frying pan, heat a little vegetable oil until hot, but not smoking. Add the patties and sear them over a high heat for about 3 minutes per side until well done. Keep the first patties warm while you cook the rest. Split the biscuits in half, spread each side with 1 tsp tomato butter and top each bottom half with a sausage patty. Place the other biscuit half on top and serve immediately.

Serves 8

cheese & ham mini muffins

see variations page 58

Nothing beats the smell of warm cheese muffins fresh from the oven. They will melt the heart of the strongest and tempt even the most difficult to please.

60 g (2 oz) fine cornmeal
85 g (3 oz) brown rice flour
30 g (1 oz) cornflour
2 tsp baking powder
pinch salt
60 g (2 oz) finely shredded Cheddar cheese
2 tbsp finely shredded Parmesan cheese

30 g (3 oz) ham, finely chopped
1 tbsp dried rosemary
1 large egg
9 tbsp buttermilk
3 tbsp canola oil
$\frac{1}{2}$ tsp Dijon mustard

Preheat the oven to 200°C (400°F/Gas mark 6). Line 12 baking cases in a mini muffin tin or grease with a little butter. In a large bowl, sift together the cornmeal, brown rice flour, cornflour, baking powder and salt. Add the cheeses, ham and rosemary and mix together until combined. In another bowl, whisk the egg with the buttermilk, canola oil and mustard.

Make a well in the middle of the dry ingredients and pour in the buttermilk mixture. Stir with a wooden spoon from the centre, incorporating all the flour as you stir. Do not overmix or worry about small lumps. Spoon into the baking cases and bake for about 12–15 minutes or until well risen and golden brown. Serve warm.

Makes 12

strawberry & coconut muffins

see variations page 59

These muffins are moist and bursting with the sweet ripeness of strawberries. The addition of coconut and banana keeps the texture perfect.

140 g (5 oz) white rice flour
30 g (1 oz) tapioca flour
30 g (1 oz) coconut flour
1 tbsp baking powder
1 tsp xantham gum
¼ tsp salt
30 g (1 oz) ground almonds
30 g (1 oz) cornmeal
110 g (4 oz) sugar

20 g (¾ oz) unsweetened
    shredded coconut
2 large eggs
270 ml (9 fl. oz) buttermilk
6 tbsp canola oil
2 tsp vanilla extract
1 ripe banana, mashed
170 g (6 oz) ripe strawberries,
    dried and sliced

Preheat the oven to 200°C (400°F/Gas mark 6) and line a 12-case muffin tin with paper muffin cases. In a bowl, sift together the flours, baking powder, xantham gum and salt. Stir in the ground almonds, cornmeal, sugar and coconut. In another bowl, whisk the eggs, then whisk in the buttermilk, oil and vanilla extract. Stir in the banana and strawberries.

Make a well in the centre of the dry ingredients and quickly pour in the wet ingredients. Stir quickly and lightly until just combined. Do not worry about a few dry bits or lumps. Spoon into the muffin cases and bake for 20–25 minutes until golden, firm to the touch and well risen. Serve warm or cool on a wire rack.

Makes 12

blueberry & white chocolate muffins

see variations page 60

Muffins packed with blueberries give a lovely burst of flavour as you bite into them and the white chocolate adds a sweet richness. Adding a banana keeps the muffins moist.

140 g (5 oz) white rice flour
80 g (2½ oz) cornflour
1 tbsp baking powder
pinch salt
110 g (4 oz) sugar
100 g (3½ oz) fine cornmeal
170 g (6 oz) white chocolate chips
   (or chopped white chocolate)

110 g (4 oz) fresh blueberries
2 large eggs
6 tbsp (3 oz) butter, melted and cooled
270 ml (9 fl. oz) buttermilk
2 tsp vanilla extract
1 small ripe banana, mashed

Preheat the oven to 200°C (400°F/Gas mark 6) and line a 12-case muffin tin with paper muffin cases. In a bowl, sift together the rice flour, cornflour, baking powder and salt. Stir in the sugar, cornmeal, white chocolate and blueberries. In another bowl, whisk the eggs, then whisk in the melted butter, buttermilk and vanilla extract. Stir in the mashed banana.

Make a well in the centre of the dry ingredients and quickly pour in the wet ingredients. Stir quickly and lightly until just combined. It does not matter if there are a few lumps and dry bits. Spoon quickly into the muffin cases and bake for 20–25 minutes until golden, firm to the touch and well risen. Serve warm or cool on a wire rack.

Makes 12

breakfast granola

see variations page 61

Cereal in the morning is so quick to prepare and this is baked in the oven with brown sugar, nuts and seeds. The aroma while it is cooking is heavenly.

280 g (10 oz) rolled oats
40 g (1½ oz) sesame seeds
85 g (3 oz) sunflower seeds
85 g (3 oz) pumpkin seeds
110 g (4 oz) chopped mixed nuts
60 g (2 oz) unsweetened shredded coconut

85 g (3 oz) brown sugar
150 ml (5 fl. oz) sunflower oil
150 ml (5 fl. oz) water
¼ tsp salt
1 tsp vanilla extract

Preheat the oven to 175°C (350°F/Gas mark 4).

In a large bowl, mix together the oats, seeds, nuts, coconut and brown sugar. In a medium bowl, whisk together the oil, water, salt and vanilla. Stir the oil and water mixture into the dry ingredients, mixing well and spread it in a large roasting tin or on a biscuit sheet. Bake for 20–30 minutes, stirring occasionally, until crisp and golden. Remove from the oven, allow to cool and store in an airtight container.

Serves 6–8

overnight caramel pecan french toast

see variations page 62

This is a great dish to make at holiday times when you have a houseful of guests. Prepare the night before and rouse everyone in the morning with the wonderful aroma of French toast drifting through the house.

230 g (8 oz) brown sugar
115 g (4 oz) butter
2 tbsp light golden syrup
110 g (4 oz) chopped pecans
2 seeded sandwich loaves (page 126),
    sliced into 18 slices
6 eggs, beaten

355 ml (12 fl. oz) milk
1 tsp vanilla extract
1 tbsp sugar
1½ tsp ground cinnamon
½ tsp ground nutmeg
icing sugar and maple syrup, to serve

For the caramel, mix together the brown sugar, butter and golden syrup in a medium saucepan. Heat, stirring, until melted and dissolved. Pour into an ungreased 22x33-cm (9x13-in) rectangular baking dish and sprinkle with half the pecans. Arrange half the bread slices in a single layer on top of the caramel, sprinkle with the rest of the pecans and place the remaining bread slices on top. In a large bowl, whisk the eggs, milk and vanilla and pour over the bread. Press lightly with the back of a spoon to moisten the bread. In a small bowl, mix together the sugar, cinnamon and nutmeg and sprinkle over the bread. Cover and chill for 18–24 hours. Preheat oven to 175°C (350°F/Gas mark 4). Bake, uncovered, for 30–40 minutes, until lightly browned. Leave to stand for 10 minutes. To serve, remove individual portions with a spatula and invert onto plates. Sprinkle with icing sugar. Serve with maple syrup on the side.

Serves 9

ham & cheese strata

see variations page 63

This rich, creamy and indulgent dish is great as part of a holiday brunch buffet because it can be prepared up to 24 hours in advance.

butter, for greasing
6 thick slices of seeded sandwich loaf
   (page 126)
230 g (8 oz) deli ham, chopped
110 g (4 oz) shredded Gruyère cheese
110 g (4 oz) shredded Cheddar cheese
4 green onions, roughly chopped

6 large eggs, lightly beaten
325 ml (11 fl. oz) milk
3 tbsp freshly chopped parsley
1 tbsp Dijon mustard
1 tbsp Worcestershire sauce

Grease a 1.9-l (2-quart) casserole dish with butter. Cut the bread slices into cubes. In a large bowl, mix together the bread, ham, cheeses and green onions. Add the eggs, milk, parsley, mustard and Worcestershire sauce. Stir well to combine. Pour into the casserole dish, cover and chill for 20–24 hours.

Preheat the oven to 175°C (350°F/Gas mark 4). Remove the cover from the casserole and bake for about 45 minutes or until a knife inserted in the middle comes out clean. Leave to stand for 10 minutes before serving.

Serves 6–8

variations

classic buttermilk pancakes

see base recipe page 21

classic chocolate chip buttermilk pancakes

Prepare the basic recipe. After forming each pancake in the frying pan, drop a few chocolate chips onto each one, pressing them lightly into the batter.

classic banana & walnut buttermilk pancakes

Prepare the basic recipe. After forming each pancake in the frying pan, drop a few banana slices and chopped walnuts onto each one, pressing them lightly into the batter.

classic cherry & almond buttermilk pancakes

Prepare the basic recipe, substituting almond extract for the vanilla. After forming each pancake, add several pitted and chopped cherries, pressing them lightly into the batter. Serve with 1 400-g (14-oz) tin cherry pie filling, warmed, as a sauce, instead of maple syrup.

dairy-free classic coconut pancakes

Prepare the basic recipe, replacing the buttermilk with coconut or almond milk and the butter with dairy-free margarine.

variations

pecan waffles with butterscotch sauce

see base recipe page 22

pecan waffles with strawberry sauce
Prepare the basic recipe, replacing the sauce with strawberry sauce.
Gently cook 160 g (5½ oz) chopped fresh strawberries with 70 g (2½ oz)
sugar and 1 teaspoon vanilla extract for 10 minutes. Remove from the heat,
mash and add 40 g (1½ oz) chopped fresh strawberries. Mix well, cool and
store in the fridge. Serve warm or cooled.

date & walnut waffles with butterscotch sauce
Prepare the basic recipe, replacing the pecans with walnuts. Sprinkle each
portion with a few chopped dates and the butterscotch sauce.

coconut waffles with cherry sauce
Prepare the basic recipe, replacing the pecans with unsweetened shredded
coconut. Instead of butterscotch sauce, serve with 1 400-g (14-oz.) tin
cherry pie filling. Add a large dollop of whipped cream, if desired.

dairy-free gingerbread waffles with maple syrup
Prepare the basic recipe, omitting the sauce. Replace the buttermilk in the
batter with coconut milk and the butter for cooking with canola oil. Add
1 teaspoon each of ground ginger and ground cinnamon to the waffle
batter. Serve with maple syrup.

variations

dutch apple breakfast cake

see base recipe page 25

dutch apple, cinnamon & raisin breakfast cake
Prepare the basic recipe, adding 1 teaspoon ground cinnamon and
1 tablespoon raisins to the frying pan with the apples.

dutch apple, peach & almond breakfast cake
Prepare the basic recipe, replacing 1 apple with 1 peach and the vanilla
extract with almond extract.

dutch apple, pear & pineapple breakfast cake
Prepare the basic recipe, replacing 2 apples with 1 peeled, cored and sliced
pear and 2 tablespoons well-drained tinned or fresh chopped pineapple.

dutch apple & blackberry breakfast cake
Prepare the basic recipe, replacing 1 apple with 30 g (1 oz) fresh blackberries.

dairy-free dutch apple & walnut breakfast cake
Prepare the basic recipe, replacing the butter with dairy-free margarine and
the buttermilk with almond milk. Add 2 tablespoons finely chopped walnuts
to the batter.

almond french toast with strawberry topping

see base recipe page 26

almond french toast stuffed with blueberries
Prepare the basic recipe, slicing the bread 2.5 cm (1 in) thick. Make a slit in each slice to form a pocket and fill with a few blueberries. Serve with maple syrup.

pecan french toast with peach topping
Prepare the basic recipe, replacing the almonds with chopped pecans and making a peach topping. Drain 1 425-g (15-oz.) tin of sliced peaches into a bowl. Mix peach juice with 1 tablespoon cornflour and bring to the boil. Add peaches, chopped and allow to cool.

almond french toast with blueberry topping
Prepare the basic recipe, replacing the strawberries with 450 g (1 lb.) blueberries. Add them to the syrup in the saucepan and simmer gently for 3 minutes before cooling.

almond french toast with pears & chocolate fudge sauce
Prepare the basic recipe, replacing the strawberry sauce with chocolate fudge sauce (page 254).

dairy-free almond french toast with maple syrup
Prepare the basic recipe, using brioche recipe (page 128), replacing the milk with rice milk and the butter with canola oil. Omit strawberry topping and serve sprinkled with a few almonds and maple syrup.

variations

eggs florentine

see base recipe page 29

eggs florentine with mustard hollandaise
Prepare the basic recipe, adding 1 teaspoon Dijon mustard to
the hollandaise.

eggs benedict
Prepare the basic recipe, omitting the spinach and substituting 1 slice of
bacon or ham, lightly sautéed in a little butter, on each biscuit.

norwegian eggs
Prepare the basic recipe, omitting the spinach and substituting 1 slice
of smoked salmon on each biscuit.

eggs maryland
Prepare the basic recipe, omitting the spinach and substituting
1 corn and crab fritter (page 97) on each biscuit.

variations

breakfast egg & cheese tortilla wraps

see base recipe page 30

breakfast fruit tortilla wraps
Prepare the basic recipe, omitting the eggs, pepper, onion and cheese.
Combine 230 g (8 oz) cottage cheese, 110 g (4 oz) cream cheese and
3 tablespoons apricot preserves. Divide mixture between the tortillas. Prepare
about 340 g (12 oz) of your favourite fruit and add to the tortillas. Wrap up
tightly and serve cold.

breakfast egg, sausage & apple wraps
Prepare the basic recipe, omitting the butter, pepper, half the cheese.
Dry-fry 170 g (6 oz) sausage meat in the frying pan before adding the onion
and eggs. Add 1 chopped apple with the cheese. Divide between the tortillas
and wrap.

breakfast egg, bacon & cheese wraps
Prepare the basic recipe, omitting the butter. Fry 6 strips of chopped bacon
in the frying pan before adding the rest of the ingredients.

dairy-free breakfast egg, spinach & feta wraps
Prepare the basic recipe, omitting pepper, onion and cheese. Add 30 g (1 oz)
fresh spinach and 90 g (3 oz) chopped feta (normally made with sheep's
milk or sheep and goat's milk), cook for 5 minutes. and wrap in tortillas.

variations

potato pancakes with smoked salmon

see base recipe page 32

potato & cheese pancakes with sausages
Prepare the basic recipe, adding 60 g (2 oz) grated Cheddar cheese to the potato mixture. Omit the smoked salmon and serve with pork breakfast sausages (page 34).

potato & mushroom pancakes with fried egg
Prepare the basic recipe, adding 60 g (2 oz) chopped mushrooms to the potato mixture. Omit the smoked salmon and serve with 1 or 2 fried eggs per portion.

potato & apple pancakes with soured cream
Prepare the basic recipe, replacing the onion with 1 Granny Smith apple, peeled, cored and grated. Serve with a large dollop of soured cream and the smoked salmon, if desired.

dairy-free potato & coriander pancakes with salsa
Prepare the basic recipe, replacing the hot milk with rice milk and adding 3 tablespoons freshly chopped coriander to the potato mixture. Instead of the smoked salmon, serve with tomato salsa.

variations

savoury cheese & onion hotcakes

see base recipe page 33

savoury cheese & bacon hotcakes
Prepare the basic recipe, omitting the vegetable oil. Dry-fry 4 strips of bacon, chopped, in the frying pan until golden and crisp before adding the onion. When you remove onion and bacon with a slotted spoon to cool, drain off all but 1 tablespoon oil in the frying pan.

savoury cheese, parsley & pine nut hotcakes
Prepare the basic recipe, adding 2 tablespoons freshly chopped parsley and 60 g (2 oz) pine nuts to the flour mixture.

savoury cheese, onion & oatmeal hotcakes
Prepare the basic recipe, replacing 2 tablespoons white rice flour with 2 tablespoons rolled oats.

savoury cheese, onion & chorizo hotcakes
Prepare the basic recipe, adding 170 g (6 oz) cooked and sliced chorizo to the flour mixture.

dairy-free savoury cheese & mushroom hotcakes
Prepare the basic recipe. Replace the cheese and milk with dairy-free cheese and rice milk and add 60 g (2 oz) chopped mushrooms with the onion.

variations

pork breakfast sausages

see base recipe page 34

breakfast venison & sun-dried tomato sausages
Prepare the basic recipe, replacing the pork with ground venison. Omit the ginger and add 4 tablespoons drained and chopped sun-dried tomatoes.

breakfast pork & watercress sausages
Prepare the basic recipe, adding 110 g (4 oz) finely chopped watercress.

breakfast lamb & rosemary sausages
Prepare the basic recipe, replacing the pork with lean ground lamb. Replace the ginger and mace with 2 tablespoons chopped dried rosemary.

breakfast beef & mustard sausages
Prepare the basic recipe, replacing the pork with lean ground beef and adding 2 tablespoons Dijon mustard.

breakfast boerwors sausages
Prepare the basic recipe, replacing half the pork with lean ground beef.

variations

sausage biscuits with sun-dried tomato butter

see base recipe page 37

sausage in parmesan biscuits with anchovy butter
Prepare the basic recipe, omitting the sun-dried tomatoes and substituting
1 tablespoon drained and finely chopped tinned anchovies. Serve in
Parmesan biscuits (page 138).

sausage & egg biscuits with sun-dried tomato butter
Prepare the basic recipe, adding 1 fried egg to each sausage biscuit.

sausage & onion biscuits with apple butter
Prepare the basic recipe, adding 2 tablespoons minced onion to
the sausage mixture. Replace the sun-dried tomato butter with
shop-bought apple butter.

sausage & cheese biscuits with sun-dried tomato butter
Prepare the basic recipe, topping each sausage patty with a slice of your
favourite cheese.

variations

cheese & ham mini muffins

see base recipe page 38

cheese & corn mini muffins
Prepare the basic recipe, replacing the ham with 40 g (1½ oz) whole kernel corn.

cheese & tomato mini muffins
Prepare the basic recipe, omitting the ham and substituting 2 tomatoes, skins and seeds removed and chopped.

cheese & asparagus mini muffins
Prepare the basic recipe, replacing the ham with 85 g (3 oz) cooked and chopped asparagus.

cheese & green onion mini muffins
Prepare the basic recipe, replacing the ham with 2 tablespoons finely chopped green onions.

dairy-free cheese & courgette mini muffins
Prepare the basic recipe, replacing the Cheddar and Parmesan cheeses with dairy-free Cheddar cheese and the buttermilk with coconut milk. Replace the ham with 2 tablespoons shredded courgette.

strawberry & coconut muffins

see base recipe page 41

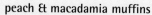

peach & macadamia muffins
Prepare the basic recipe, omitting the coconut and strawberries. Substitute 110 g (4 oz) peeled, pitted and chopped fresh peaches and 85 g (3 oz) chopped macadamia nuts.

apricot & almond muffins
Prepare the basic recipe, omitting the coconut, strawberries and vanilla extract. Replace with 110 g (4 oz) peeled, pitted and chopped fresh or tinned apricots, 90 g (3 oz) chopped almonds and 1 teaspoon almond extract.

chocolate chip, pecan & coconut muffins
Prepare the basic recipe, replacing the strawberries with 170 g (6 oz) plain chocolate chips and 90 g (3 oz) chopped pecans.

dairy-free pumpkin pie & walnut muffins
Prepare the basic recipe, omitting the buttermilk, banana, coconut and strawberries. Replace with 90 ml (3 fl. oz) coconut milk, 170 g (6 oz) tinned pumpkin, 90 g (3 oz) chopped walnuts, 1 teaspoon ground cinnamon and 1 teaspoon pumpkin pie spice. Just before baking, top each muffin with half a walnut and when cool, glaze with a little maple syrup.

blueberry & white chocolate muffins

see base recipe page 42

orange & chocolate chip muffins
Prepare the basic recipe, omitting the blueberries and white chocolate.
Substitute 2 teaspoons shredded orange zest and 170 g (6 oz) chopped
orange-flavoured milk chocolate or milk chocolate chips.

apple & cinnamon muffins
Omit the blueberries and white chocolate. Substitute 110 g (4 oz) peeled,
cored and grated apple and 1 teaspoon cinnamon.

cherry, coconut & white chocolate muffins
Omit the blueberries and ¼ of the white chocolate. Substitute 110 g (4 oz)
pitted and chopped cherries and 20 g (¾ oz) shredded coconut.

carrot & pineapple muffins
Omit the blueberries, white chocolate and banana. Substitute 85 g (3 oz)
finely shredded carrot and 110 g (4 oz) well-drained crushed pineapple.

dairy-free raspberry muffins
Prepare the basic recipe, omitting the butter, buttermilk, blueberries and
white chocolate. Substitute dairy-free margarine, coconut milk and 110 g
(4 oz) fresh raspberries.

variations

breakfast granola

see base recipe page 45

very berry breakfast granola with raspberries & maple syrup
Prepare the basic recipe, adding 60 g (2 oz) mixed dried berries to the granola
when it is fresh from the oven. Serve sprinkled with fresh raspberries and
drizzled with maple syrup.

gingerbread breakfast granola
Prepare the basic recipe, adding 3 teaspoons ground ginger and 1 teaspoon
ground cinnamon to the dry ingredients.

macadamia breakfast granola
Prepare the basic recipe, replacing the mixed nuts with 60 g (2 oz) coarsely
chopped macadamia nuts and 85 g (3 oz) golden raisins.

apple & almond breakfast granola
Prepare the basic recipe, replacing the mixed nuts with chopped almonds and
the vanilla with almond extract. Add 170 g (6 oz) chopped dried apple rings to
the cereal when it is fresh from the oven.

date & walnut breakfast granola
Prepare the basic recipe, replacing the mixed nuts with chopped walnuts.
Add 85 g (3 oz) chopped dried dates to cereal when it is fresh from the oven.

variations

overnight caramel pecan french toast

see base recipe page 46

overnight caramel, banana & walnut french toast
Prepare the basic recipe, replacing the pecans with walnuts and adding 2 sliced bananas to the first layer of bread in the dish.

overnight caramel, pear & chocolate chip french toast
Prepare the basic recipe, adding 60 g (2 oz) peeled, cored and chopped fresh or tinned pear and 85 g (3 oz) plain chocolate chips, scattered over the first layer of bread in the dish.

overnight caramel, apricot & almond french toast
Prepare the basic recipe, replacing the pecans with sliced almonds and the vanilla extract with almond extract. Add 60 g (2 oz) drained and chopped tinned apricots to the first layer of bread in the dish.

dairy-free overnight caramel, pineapple & coconut french toast
Prepare the basic recipe, replacing the butter and milk with dairy-free margarine and almond milk. Add 60 g (2 oz) well-drained crushed pineapple and 30 g (1 oz) unsweetened shredded coconut to the first layer of bread in the dish.

ham & cheese strata

see base recipe page 47

bacon & tomato strata
Prepare the basic recipe, replacing the ham with cooked bacon and adding
4 seeded and chopped tomatoes.

sausage & pepper strata
Prepare the basic recipe, replacing the ham with cooked sausage and adding
$\frac{1}{2}$ red pepper, sliced.

mexican strata with chillis
Prepare the basic recipe, replacing the ham with chopped cooked chorizo and
adding 2 seeded and chopped tomatoes and 1 or 2 finely chopped chillis.

crabmeat strata
Prepare the basic recipe, replacing the ham with 340 g (12 oz) tinned or fresh
(picked over) crabmeat.

dairy-free tuna niçoise strata
Prepare the basic recipe, replacing the cheeses and milk with 110 g (4 oz) dairy-
free Cheddar cheese and rice milk. Replace the ham with 170 g (6 oz) tinned
tuna, drained and add 2 seeded and chopped tomatoes and a few pitted and
halved black olives.

appetisers &
starters

The dishes in this chapter are very versatile.

They are suitable with before-dinner drinks, for

whetting the appetite before a dinner party,

or as a light meal in the middle of the day or

supper at night.

tomato bruschetta

see variations page 94

The garlic, basil and olive oil with the tomatoes are a classic Mediterranean combination. This is a quick starter to prepare.

6–7 Roma (plum) tomatoes
3 tbsp finely chopped red onion
2 large cloves garlic, minced
2 tbsp freshly chopped basil leaves
2–3 tbsp olive oil
$\frac{1}{2}$ tsp cider vinegar

salt and freshly ground black pepper
$\frac{1}{2}$ tsp sugar
4 soft dinner rolls (page 116)
few sprigs fresh coriander or basil, to serve

First, remove the tomato skins. Score each tomato around the middle with a knife and place in a large bowl. Cover with boiling water and leave for 3 minutes. Drain away the water and slide off the skins, being careful as they will be hot. Slice the tomatoes in half and remove the seeds by running your finger around the inside.

Chop the tomatoes into a medium bowl with the onion, garlic, 1 tablespoon olive oil, cider vinegar, salt, pepper and sugar. Mix well to combine. Cover and chill for about an hour. Preheat the grill. Slice the rolls in half horizontally. Brush both sides of each roll half with a little olive oil, then grill both sides for a minute or so or until lightly browned. Arrange on a serving plate and spoon the tomato mixture onto the bread, dividing it equally. Garnish with a few sprigs of coriander or basil and serve immediately.

Makes 8 slices

blue cheese-stuffed mushrooms

see variations page 95

Portobello mushrooms, filled with a mixture of shallots, mushrooms, blue cheese and breadcrumbs, are baked in the oven until the cheese just starts to brown. You can prepare them ahead of time and bake just before needed.

6 large flat portobello mushrooms
60 g (2 oz) butter
2 shallots, finely chopped
170 g (6 oz) crumbled blue cheese

30 g (1 oz) breadcrumbs or coarse cornmeal
1 tbsp freshly chopped parsley
salt and freshly ground black pepper

Preheat the oven to 175°C (350°F/Gas mark 4). Carefully remove the stalks from the mushrooms. Chop stalks finely. Wipe the caps with damp paper towels.

In a medium frying pan, melt half the butter, add the mushroom stalks and shallots and cook for 5–7 minutes, until softened. Remove from the heat and allow to cool for 5 minutes. Add the blue cheese, breadcrumbs, parsley and salt and pepper to taste.

Put the rest of the butter into a shallow baking dish and place in the oven for 3 minutes to heat. Divide the cheese mixture between the mushroom caps and place in the baking dish. Bake for 20 minutes until heated through and the cheese is just starting to brown.

Serves 4

lamb koftas

see variations page 96

Rolled in fresh parsley and mint, these delicious lamb kebabs can be grilled, cooked on a griddle or grilled outside on the barbecue.

510 g (1 lb 2 oz) lean ground lamb
1 tsp ground cumin
2 tsp ground coriander
1 tbsp freshly chopped coriander
1 tbsp freshly chopped mint
1 tbsp chickpea flour

2 cloves garlic, minced
salt and freshly ground black pepper
oil, for brushing
2 tbsp freshly chopped parsley
2 tbsp freshly chopped mint

In a large bowl, with your hands, mix the lamb, cumin, ground coriander, chopped coriander, mint, flour, garlic and salt and pepper. Make sure the herbs and spices are evenly distributed throughout the mixture. Form into 8 balls, then roll with your hands into ovals.

Press onto 4 metal skewers, 2 on each one, tamping the meat around the skewers. Mix the chopped parsley and mint together on a plate. Brush the koftas with oil and roll in the parsley and mint. Chill until ready to cook.

Preheat the grill, barbecue or griddle. Cook for 3–4 minutes per side, until cooked through. Serve immediately with tzatkiki (page 96).

Serves 4

corn fritters

see variations page 97

The ingredients in the fritters are probably all in your kitchen, so this is something you can throw together at the last minute. Crisp on the outside and with a tempting texture, serve these little fritters with sweet chilli sauce (page 194).

340 g (12 oz) whole kernel sweetcorn,
    fresh or frozen
2 eggs, lightly beaten
1 large banana, mashed
4 tbsp chopped green onions
1 tsp ground cumin
1 tbsp freshly chopped coriander
½ tsp crushed dried red chilli flakes

salt and freshly ground black pepper
70 g (2½ oz) white rice flour
65 g (2¼ oz) brown rice flour
1 tsp baking powder
4–6 tbsp vegetable oil, for frying
spinach leaves, chopped tomatoes and chilli
    sauce, to serve

In a large bowl, put the corn, egg and mashed banana. Add the green onions, cumin, coriander and red chilli flakes. Season with salt and pepper. Stir in the flours and baking powder and fold together lightly to form a loose batter.

In a large frying pan heat the oil and when it is hot, but not smoking, drop tablespoons of the mixture into the oil, one at a time and fry for 1–2 minutes per side until lightly golden. Remove from the tin with a slotted spoon and drain on paper towels, keeping them warm while you cook the rest. To serve, arrange a few fresh spinach leaves and chopped tomatoes on a serving plate and place the fritters on top, with a small bowl of sweet chilli sauce on the side.

Serves 4–6

falafels with tzatziki

see variations page 98

A low-calorie choice for a starter, these are crispy on the outside and soft on the inside. They are especially delicious with tzatziki, a mint yogurt sauce.

1 500 g (16-oz) tin chickpeas, well drained
1 medium onion, finely chopped
2 cloves garlic, crushed
½ tsp harissa paste
3 tbsp freshly chopped parsley

1 tsp ground coriander
1 tsp ground cumin
2 tbsp chickpea flour
salt and freshly ground black pepper
vegetable oil, for deep-frying

Dry the chickpeas with paper towels. Place all the ingredients, except the vegetable oil, into a food processor and pulse until well combined. (You could also mash the chickpeas in a bowl, with a fork, then mix in the rest of the ingredients.) Form the mixture into 4 balls.

In a medium saucepan, pour in oil to about 8 cm (3 in) deep. When the oil is hot, but not smoking, add the falafels and deep-fry for 3–4 minutes, until golden brown. Drain on paper towels for 2 minutes. Serve with tzatziki (page 96).

Serves 4–6

spicy squash & carrot soup

see variations page 99

There is nothing better than a warming bowl of spicy soup on a chilly day in the autumn. Even the colour reflects the season.

1 medium-size butternut squash
2 large carrots
2 tbsp olive oil
1 large onion, finely chopped
3 cloves garlic, crushed
1 tsp ground cumin

2 tbsp fresh thyme leaves
2 tsp dried red chilli flakes
1 l (40 fl. oz) good-quality chicken stock
salt and freshly ground black pepper
2 tbsp grated Parmesan cheese, to serve

Peel the squash, remove the seeds and chop the flesh into 2.5-cm (1-in) chunks. Peel and slice the carrots. Set both aside.

In a large saucepan, over a medium heat, heat olive oil and add the onion and garlic. Cook for 5 minutes until softened. Stir in the cumin, thyme, red chilli flakes, squash, carrots and chicken stock. Cover and simmer gently for 45 minutes, until the vegetables have softened.

Season with salt and pepper to taste. Allow to cool slightly, then blend in a blender until smooth. When ready to serve, return soup to saucepan to reheat until piping hot and serve immediately, sprinkled with a little Parmesan.

Serves 6

rice & cheese patties

see variations page 100

These little patties will melt in your mouth.

250 g (9 oz) long-grain rice
1 tbsp olive oil, plus a little extra
6 spring onions, sliced
170 g (6 oz) shredded Cheddar cheese

1 tsp Dijon mustard
salt and freshly ground black pepper
50 g (1³/₄ oz) white rice flour
chopped spring onions, to serve

In a large saucepan, place the rice, cover with water and bring to the boil. Simmer gently for 10 minutes. Drain but do not rinse, as the rice should be a little sticky. Set aside. In a large frying pan, heat 1 tablespoon oil, add the onions and cook for 2 minutes, until softened. Remove from the heat and transfer the onions with a slotted spoon to a large bowl. Add the rice, cheese and Dijon mustard to the onions and season with salt and pepper.

Mix the rice flour on a plate with salt and pepper. With wet hands, shape the cooked rice mixture into 12 patties and roll in the seasoned rice flour to coat. Add a little more oil to the frying pan and cook the patties in batches, over a medium heat, for a few minutes on each side, until golden brown and cooked through. Drain on paper towels and keep warm while you cook the rest. Serve sprinkled with a few chopped spring onions.

Makes 12 patties

cheese & chorizo quesadillas

see variations page 101

These are a taste explosion in every bite. Make plenty, as they will disappear really fast.

110 g (4 oz) shredded mozzarella
110 g (4 oz) shredded Monterey Jack cheese
230 g (8 oz) chorizo, casing removed, chopped
4 spring onions, finely chopped
2 fresh green chillies, seeded and finely
    chopped

salt and freshly ground black pepper
10 corn tortillas
1 tbsp vegetable oil, plus extra if needed
soured cream and avocado salsa (page 100),
    to serve

In a large bowl, place the cheeses, chorizo, green onions and chillies. Season with salt and pepper. Divide the mixture between 5 tortillas and place the other 5 on top.

In a large frying pan, heat 1 tablespoon vegetable oil and when it is hot, but not smoking, add a quesadilla. Cook, pressing down with a spatula, for about 5 minutes. The underside should be crisp and lightly browned. Turn the quesadilla over and cook the other side until the cheese has melted. Remove from the frying pan and keep warm while you cook the rest, adding more oil to the frying pan as necessary. Serve with soured cream and avocado salsa.

Makes 5 quesadillas

salmon tempura

see variations page 102

A Japanese-influenced dish, tempura batter should be light and airy, crunchy and without any trace of oiliness. Make the batter just before using it.

for the dipping sauce
60 ml (2 fl. oz) soya sauce
60 ml (2 fl. oz) Chinese wine (mirin)
1 tsp horseradish sauce

230 g (8 oz) salmon fillet, skinned and boned
salt and freshly ground black pepper
60 g (2 oz) cornflour
70 g (2½ oz) white rice flour
240 ml (8 fl. oz) ice cold carbonated water
35 g (1¼ oz) white rice flour for the salmon
sunflower oil, for frying

Make the dipping sauce by mixing together the soya sauce, mirin and horseradish sauce in a small bowl. Set aside.

Cut the salmon into large bite-size pieces. Sprinkle with salt and pepper. In a large bowl, mix together the cornflour, rice flour and more salt. Add just enough soda water to make a thick batter. Do not over mix or worry about small lumps.

In a large saucepan or wok, heat about 8 cm (3 in) oil until hot but not smoking. Dip the salmon first in rice flour and then in the batter. Drop into the oil. Do not overcrowd the pan and cook for 2 or 3 minutes. Remove with a slotted spoon and keep warm while you cook the rest. Serve with the dipping sauce on the side.

Serves 4–6

onion bhajis with chickpea flour

see variations page 103

Usually this would be a starter to an Indian-themed dinner, but it makes a wonderful appetiser before any meal.

2 tsp cumin seeds
2 tsp coriander seeds
2 green chillies
3 cloves garlic, crushed
1 tsp salt
2 tsp finely chopped fresh root ginger

230 g (8 oz) chickpea flour
1 tsp ground turmeric
2 large onions, finely sliced
3 large courgettes, coarsely shredded
2–3 tbsp ice water
canola oil for deep-frying

Crush the cumin and coriander seeds in a pestle and mortar or with the back of a spoon. In a large bowl, mix the spices with the chillies, garlic, salt, ginger, flour, turmeric, onions and courgettes. Stir in enough ice water to give the mixture a soft dropping consistency. (This is when the mixture holds together, but drops off the spoon with a heavy lump.) Do not add too much water or the bhajis will be hard to fry.

Heat 8 cm (3 in) of oil in a medium saucepan. When it is hot, but not smoking, drop in the batter a spoonful at a time and cook for about 5 minutes or until golden brown. Do not overcrowd the pan. Remove with a slotted spoon and drain on kitchen towel. Keep warm while you cook the rest. Serve with tzatziki (page 96).

Serves 4

wild mushroom & crème fraîche tart

see variations page 104

Mushrooms, onions and garlic are always a good combination and when mixed with crème fraîche, even better.

1 20-cm (9-in) GF pastry crust (page 17)
5 tbsp (2½ oz) butter
2 large onions, sliced
60 g (2 oz) brown sugar
6 tbsp red wine vinegar
2 cloves garlic, crushed

350–450 g (12 oz–1 lb) sliced mixed wild and
    cultivated mushrooms, such as shitake,
    oyster, button and field
3 tbsp freshly chopped parsley
240 ml (8 fl. oz) crème fraîche
4 eggs, lightly beaten
salt and freshly ground black pepper

Blind bake the pastry in a 20-cm (9-in) loose-bottomed fluted tart tin. While it bakes, make the filling. In a large frying pan, melt 3 tablespoons butter and fry the onions for 20 minutes over a medium heat. Increase the heat and fry for a further 8–10 minutes, until lightly browned. Stir in the sugar and vinegar and simmer for 5 minutes, until the vinegar has reduced and the mixture has a jam-like consistency. Remove from the heat and set aside. In another frying pan, melt the remaining butter, add the garlic and mushrooms and cook gently for about 5 minutes, stirring occasionally. Remove from the heat and add the parsley.

Leave to stand for 5 minutes. Reduce the oven temperature to 190°C (375°F/Gas mark 5) and spread the onion mixture in the pastry shell. Drain the mushrooms of and scatter them over the onions.

In a large bowl, beat the eggs and crème fraîche together until smooth. Season well with salt and pepper, then pour carefully into the pastry shell, discarding any excess mixture. Bake for 25 minutes, until golden brown and set. Cool slightly, remove carefully from the tin and serve immediately.

Serves 4–6

cod & haddock fish cakes

see variations page 105

Fish cakes are at their best when the middle is soft and the outside crunchy. They are filling, low-calorie and good value for money.

230 g (8 oz) cod fillet, skinned and boned
230 g (8 oz) haddock fillet, skinned and boned
240 ml (8 fl. oz) milk
2–3 bay leaves
340 g (12 oz) potatoes
1 tbsp thick cream
1 tsp lemon zest
2 tbsp freshly chopped parsley

salt and freshly ground black pepper
35 g (1^1/$_5$ oz) white rice flour
1 egg, beaten
130 g (4^1/$_2$ oz) coarse cornmeal
4 tbsp vegetable oil
watercress, lemon wedges and mayonnaise,
    to serve

In a large frying pan, place the fish, add the milk and bay leaf, cover and bring to the boil. Lower the heat and simmer for 5 minutes. Remove from the heat and leave to stand for 10 minutes. Then lift the fish out of the milk with a slotted spoon and place on a plate to cool slightly.

Meanwhile, peel the potatoes and cut into chunks. Put into a large saucepan, cover with boiling water and simmer for about 15 minutes or until tender. Drain and allow to cool for 2–3 minutes in the colander. Tip back into the saucepan and put them over the lowest heat possible for 2 minutes to dry. Mash with a fork until they are light and fluffy. Beat in the cream, lemon zest and parsley. Season with plenty of salt and pepper.

Pat the fish dry with kitchen towel and flake it into the potato in large pieces. Fold it in lightly, trying not to break up the fish too much. Set aside to cool.

Put the rice flour on a large plate, the egg on a second plate and the cornmeal on a third. Dust your hands with rice flour and form 4 fish cakes about 2.5 cm (1 in) deep. Dredge them in rice flour first, then coat all over in the egg. Lift into the cornmeal and dredge them all over, patting the cornmeal onto the top and sides. Transfer to a clean plate, cover and chill for 30 minutes to 24 hours.

In a large frying pan, heat the vegetable oil. When it is hot but not smoking, fry the fish cakes for about 5 minutes per side or until crisp and golden. Serve immediately with a little watercress, some lemon wedges and a little mayonnaise.

Serves 4

cheese soufflé

see variations page 106

Ideal for a starter or lunch, this soufflé should be quickly made and quickly eaten.

melted butter, for brushing
2 tbsp (1 oz) butter
2 tbsp (1 oz) white rice flour
150 ml (5 fl. oz) hot milk
60 g (2 oz) shredded Cheddar cheese

½ tsp Dijon mustard
salt and freshly ground black pepper
3 egg yolks
4 egg whites

Brush the inside of a 1-l (1½-pint) or 15-cm (6-in) soufflé dish with melted butter. Cut a strip of doubled baking parchment, long enough to go around the outside of the dish, overlapping by 3–5 cm (1–2 in) and 2–8 cm (1–2 in) higher than the dish. Tape or tie the strip securely around the dish. Where paper extends above the dish, brush with melted butter. Preheat oven to 190°C (375°F/Gas mark 5).

In a large saucepan, melt the butter, stir in the flour and cook, stirring for 2 minutes. Remove from the heat and very gradually add the hot milk, stirring continuously until combined. Return the tin to the heat and slowly bring to the boil, stirring constantly until thickened. Lower the heat and add the cheese, mustard, salt and pepper. Remove from the heat and allow to cool. Beat in the egg yolks. Place a baking tray on the middle shelf of the oven. In a clean bowl, whisk the egg whites until stiff. Fold 2 tablespoons of egg whites into the cooled sauce with a metal spoon, to loosen it, then fold in the rest of the egg whites, making a figure-eight pattern with the spoon. Make sure you bring up the sauce from the bottom of the pan. Spoon the mixture into the prepared soufflé dish, place on the baking tray and bake for 30–35 minutes or until set and golden brown. Serve immediately.

Serves 4–6

chicken satay with peanut sauce

see variations page 107

If you are looking for a different way to prepare chicken, look no further. The peanut sauce is spicy without being too hot and the chicken can be cooked on the barbecue instead of under the grill, if desired.

for the chicken
3 skinless and boneless chicken breasts
1 tbsp honey
1 tbsp soya sauce
pinch cayenne pepper
1 clove garlic, crushed
1 tsp finely chopped fresh root ginger

for the peanut sauce
2 cloves garlic, crushed
2 tsp finely chopped fresh root ginger
1 tsp ground cumin
1 tsp ground coriander
2 tbsp freshly squeezed lime juice
2 tbsp light brown sugar
1 tsp red chilli paste
230 g (8 oz) smooth peanut butter
2 tbsp water

Cut the chicken into strips and set aside. In a large bowl, mix the honey, soya sauce, pepper, garlic and root ginger. Add the chicken. Turn the chicken around in the marinade, cover, and chill for at least an hour, preferably several. To make the peanut sauce, place all the ingredients in a food processor and pulse several times until well blended. If the sauce seems too thick, add a little more water. Transfer to a serving bowl and chill, covered.

Preheat the grill. Remove the chicken from the marinade and thread onto metal skewers in a rough 'S' shape. Place about 8 cm (3 in) from the grill and grill for about 3–4 minutes per side, until cooked through but still tender. Serve immediately with the peanut sauce.

Makes 6

smoked mackerel pâté

see variations page 108

Mackerel is full of flavour and health-giving omega-3 fatty acids. Add the horseradish sauce to taste, as some are stronger than others.

3 fillets (about 230 g (8 oz)) smoked mackerel,
    skinned and boned
70 g (2½ oz) cream cheese
70 g (2½ oz) soured cream
1 tbsp lemon juice or to taste

2 tsp horseradish sauce or to taste
salt and freshly ground black pepper
toasted seeded sandwich loaf (page 126),
    to serve

Carefully check there are no small bones in the fish. Place all the ingredients in a food processor and pulse a few times until well combined. Season with salt and pepper and add a little more lemon juice or horseradish to taste. Transfer the pâté to a serving bowl, cover and chill for 4 hours to 4 days. To serve, spread on toasted bread slices.

Serves 4

aubergine stuffed with crab

see variations page 109

Wow your friends with aubergines stuffed with onion, tomato and flaked crab, which make an unusual appetiser or light lunch.

2 aubergines (each about 15 cm long)
salt
1 tbsp vegetable oil, plus extra for cooking
2 medium onions, thinly sliced
2 tsp paprika
1 tbsp tomato paste
230 g (8 oz) ripe tomatoes, skinned, seeded and
    sliced

1 tsp dried oregano
pinch cayenne pepper
freshly ground black pepper
170–200 g (6–7 oz) crabmeat, tinned or fresh,
    picked over
2 tbsp grated Parmesan cheese
2 tbsp shredded Gruyère cheese
1–2 tbsp (1 oz) butter, melted

Split the aubergines in half lengthwise, score the flesh, sprinkle with salt and leave for 30 minutes. Preheat the oven to 175°C (350°F/Gas mark 4). In a large frying pan, heat 1 tablespoon vegetable oil. Wipe the aubergines dry, brown the cut surface, remove and place on a greased baking tray. Cook in the oven for about 10 minutes, until tender. Add a little more oil to the frying pan and cook the onions for 5 minutes until softened. Add the paprika, tomato paste, tomatoes oregano and cayenne. Season to taste with salt and pepper and continue to cook over low heat until the mixture becomes a rich pulp, about 10–15 minutes.

Remove aubergines from the oven and turn up the heat to 220°C (425°F/Gas mark 7). Scoop out the flesh from the cooked aubergines, chop and add to the mixture in the frying pan. Cook for 5 minutes. Flake the crabmeat, add to the frying pan and mix well. Pile mixture into the aubergine skins, sprinkle with the cheeses and melted butter. Bake in the oven for about 6–7 minutes until browned.

Serves 4

variations

tomato bruschetta

see base recipe page 65

mixed tomato & coriander bruschetta
Prepare the basic recipe, replacing the Roma tomatoes with a selection of tomatoes in different colours – yellow, green and orange. Replace the basil with coriander.

tuna, tomato & olive bruschetta
Prepare the basic recipe, adding 60 g (2 oz) drained, tinned tuna and 2 tablespoons pitted and chopped black olives to the tomato mixture.

mexican bruschetta
Prepare the basic recipe, adding 2 medium chillies, seeded and finely chopped, to the tomato mixture. Replace the basil with coriander.

ham & tomato bruschetta
Prepare the basic recipe, adding a slice of deli ham to each roll half before spooning on the tomato mixture.

variations

blue cheese-stuffed mushrooms

see base recipe page 66

blue cheese & spinach-stuffed mushrooms
Prepare the basic recipe, adding 40 g (1½ oz) cooked chopped spinach to the mixture in the frying pan.

blue cheese-stuffed mushrooms with cranberry relish
Prepare the basic recipe. Make the cranberry relish by combining 2 tablespoons olive oil, 1 small finely chopped red onion, 3 tablespoons red wine, 1 tablespoon cider vinegar, 7 tablespoons brown sugar, 1 tablespoon redcurrant jam and 60 g (2 oz) cranberries in a medium saucepan. Cook for 7 minutes. Serve warm or cold.

truffle-scented blue cheese-stuffed mushrooms
Prepare the basic recipe, replacing the olive oil with truffle-scented oil.

blue cheese & parma ham stuffed mushrooms
Prepare the basic recipe, adding 60 g (2 oz) chopped parma ham to the mixture in the frying pan.

blue cheese & sun-dried tomato stuffed mushrooms
Prepare the basic recipe, adding 60 g (2 oz) chopped sun-dried tomatoes to the mixture in the frying pan.

variations

lamb koftas

see base recipe page 69

lamb koftas with turmeric & paprika
Prepare the basic recipe, replacing the ground cumin and coriander with
2 teaspoons ground turmeric and 1 teaspoon paprika.

lamb koftas with tzatziki
Prepare the basic recipe. Serve with tzatziki, made by mixing 340 g (12 oz)
Greek-style yogurt with ½ cucumber, coarsely grated; 2 cloves garlic,
minced; 1 tablespoon lemon juice; 1 tablespoon freshly chopped mint;
and 1 teaspoon olive oil. Can be made ahead and chilled or made and
served immediately.

lamb & fruit koftas
Prepare the basic recipe, adding 2 tablespoons raisins to the lamb mixture.

tafta koftas
Prepare the basic recipe, replacing the lamb with lean ground beef. Form
mixture into 10–12 meatballs, heat 2 tablespoons olive oil in a large frying
pan and fry for about 15 minutes, until cooked through. Serve with tzatziki
(see above) and rice, if desired.

variations

corn fritters

see base recipe page 70

corn & crab fritters
Prepare the basic recipe, replacing 85 g (3 oz) corn with 85 g (3 oz) tinned or
picked-over fresh crab. Replace the coriander with parsley.

corn & avocado fritters
Prepare the basic recipe, replacing the banana with 1 ripe avocado, peeled,
pitted and finely chopped.

pea fritters
Prepare the basic recipe, replacing the corn with frozen peas.

corn & pepper fritters
Prepare the basic recipe, adding 1 tablespoon each of finely chopped red and
green peppers to the mixture before cooking.

thai corn fritters
Prepare the basic recipe, adding 1 teaspoon freshly chopped root ginger and
2 teaspoons red Thai curry paste to the mixture before cooking.

variations

falafels with tzatziki

see base recipe page 73

falafel patties with coriander
Prepare the basic recipe, replacing the parsley with coriander. Form the falafels into patties and shallow-fry for 3–4 minutes per side. Serve wrapped up in corn tortillas with chopped cucumber and tomato.

falafel patties with hummus
Prepare the basic recipe. Make hummus by draining 1 500 g (16-oz) tin chickpeas, saving the juice. In a food processor, blend the chickpeas with 60 ml (2 fl. oz) chickpea juice, 4 tablespoons lemon juice, 4 teaspoons tahini paste, 2 crushed cloves garlic, 2 teaspoons paprika, ½ teaspoon salt, and 3–4 tablespoons olive oil. Omit the tzatziki.

falafels with pine nuts
Prepare the basic recipe, adding 40 g (1½ oz) pine nuts to the mixture.

fava bean falafel
Prepare the basic recipe, replacing the chickpeas with fava beans and the parsley with coriander.

variations

spicy squash & carrot soup

see base recipe page 74

spicy squash & potato soup
Prepare the basic recipe, adding 230 g (8 oz) peeled and chopped potatoes to the pan with the vegetables.

curry squash & parsnip soup
Prepare the basic recipe, adding 1 or 2 peeled and chopped parsnips and 2 teaspoons curry powder to the pan with the vegetables. Replace the parsley and Parmesan garnish with freshly chopped coriander.

spicy squash soup with cheese croutons
Prepare the basic recipe. Make cheese croutons with 240 ml (8 fl. oz) cheese sauce (page 224) spread on slices of toasted seeded sandwich loaf (page 126). Sprinkle plenty of grated Cheddar cheese on top and brown under the grill. Cut into strips and serve hot with the soup.

spicy squash & pasta soup
Prepare the basic recipe. 20 minutes before the end of cooking time, add 110 g (4 oz) dried pasta shells to the pan. Serve without blending.

variations

rice & cheese patties

see base recipe page 77

rice & cheese patties with chilli peppers
Prepare the basic recipe, adding 2 tablespoons freshly chopped coriander
and 1 finely chopped chilli to the mixture.

rice & cheese patties with prawns
Prepare the basic recipe, adding 85 g (3 oz) cooked, chopped prawns.

rice & cheese patties with avocado salsa
Prepare the basic recipe and serve with avocado salsa. Peel, pit and chop
1 avocado. Mix with 2 peeled and seeded tomatoes, 1/2 finely chopped
small red onion, 1 tablespoon freshly chopped coriander, 2 tablespoons
freshly squeezed lime juice, pinch dried red chilli flakes, 1 teaspoon
sugar and salt and freshly squeezed black pepper. Serve immediately.

rice, asparagus & cheese patties
Prepare the basic recipe, adding 85 g (3 oz) cooked and chopped asparagus
to the mixture.

rice, tomato & cheese patties
Prepare the basic recipe, adding 1 tomato, peeled and seeded, to
the mixture.

cheese & chorizo quesadillas

see base recipe page 79

cheese & bean quesadillas
Prepare the basic recipe, replacing the chorizo with 170 g (6 oz) black beans.

spinach & mushroom quesadillas
Prepare the basic recipe, omitting the chorizo. Substitute 90 g (3 oz) cooked, cooled and chopped spinach and 85 g (3 oz) chopped mushrooms that have been sautéed for 5 minutes in a little butter.

goat cheese & asparagus quesadillas
Prepare the basic recipe, omitting the mozzarella and chorizo. Replace with 110 g (4 oz) chopped goat's cheese and 170 g (6 oz) cooked and chopped asparagus.

chicken & mango quesadillas
Prepare the basic recipe, replacing the chorizo with chopped cooked chicken. Add 60 g (2 oz) chopped ripe mango to the mixture.

cheese & caramelised onion quesadillas
Prepare the basic recipe, omitting the chorizo. Fry 2 sliced onions gently in 2 tablespoons oil for about 20 minutes, then add 3 tablespoons brown sugar and cook for another 10 minutes, until caramelised. Add to the quesadillas.

variations

salmon tempura

see base recipe page 80

prawn tempura
Prepare the basic recipe, adding 30 g (1 oz) unsweetened shredded coconut
to the batter and replacing the salmon with large prawns, deveined and
heads removed. Dip in the batter, leaving the tails exposed.

courgette tempura
Prepare the basic recipe, replacing the salmon with 230 g (8 oz) courgettes,
sliced into thin strips.

mahi mahi tempura
Prepare the basic recipe, replacing the salmon with 230 g (8 oz)
mahi mahi.

sweet potato tempura
Prepare the basic recipe, replacing the salmon with 230 g (8 oz) peeled
sweet potato, cut into thin strips.

mushroom tempura
Prepare the basic recipe, replacing the salmon with 230 g (8 oz)
mushrooms, sliced.

onion bhajis with chickpea flour

see base recipe page 83

cauliflower & onion bhajis with chickpea flour
Prepare the basic recipe, replacing half the onion with 230 g (8 oz) cauliflower florets.

carrot & celery bhajis with chickpea flour
Prepare the basic recipe, replacing the onions with 230 g (8 oz) peeled and thinly sliced carrots and 230 g (8 oz) sliced celery.

potato & onion bhajis with chickpea flour
Prepare the basic recipe, replacing 1 onion with 230 g (8 oz) potatoes, peeled and very thinly sliced.

pepper & onion bhajis with chickpea flour
Prepare the basic recipe, replacing 1 onion with 2 peppers, seeded and thinly sliced.

mushroom & onion bhajis with chickpea flour
Prepare the basic recipe, replacing two-thirds of the onion with 60 g (2 oz) thinly sliced mushrooms.

wild mushroom & crème fraîche tart

see base recipe page 84

wild mushroom, bacon & crème fraîche tart
Prepare the basic recipe, adding 4 strips cooked and finely chopped bacon to the onion mixture.

wild mushroom, prawn & crème fraîche tart
Prepare the basic recipe, adding 40 g (1½ oz) cooked prawns to the pastry shell with the onion mixture.

wild mushroom, asparagus & crème fraîche tart
Prepare the basic recipe, adding 40 g (1½ oz) cooked and chopped asparagus to the pastry shell with the onion mixture.

wild mushroom, parmesan & crème fraîche tart
Prepare the basic recipe, adding 30 g (1 oz) shredded Parmesan to the pastry shell with the onion mixture.

wild mushroom, italian sausage & crème fraîche tart
Prepare the basic recipe, adding 40 g (1½ oz) chopped and cooked Italian sausage to the pastry shell with the onion mixture.

variations

cod & haddock fish cakes

see base recipe page 86

cod & tilapia fish cakes with tartar sauce
Prepare the basic recipe, replacing the haddock with tilapia. Make tartar
sauce by mixing 170 g (6 oz) mayonnaise with 2 tablespoons drained
and chopped capers, 2 tablespoons drained and chopped mini gherkins,
1 teaspoon lemon juice, 3 tablespoons freshly chopped parsley and salt
and freshly ground black pepper in a small bowl. Chill until ready to serve.

thai crab cakes
Instead of the basic recipe, pulse 1 100-g (3½-oz) packet of rice crackers in a
food processor until very fine. Put half onto a plate. Add to the processor
340 g (12 oz) crab meat. Chop 2 chillies, 6 green onions, 4 kaffir lime leaves
and a small bunch coriander. Add to processor with 4 tablespoons
mayonnaise, 3 teaspoons fish sauce and 2 beaten eggs. Pulse until mixed,
form into cakes, roll in the rice crackers and fry for 4 minutes each side.

salmon fish cakes
Prepare the basic recipe, replacing the cod and haddock with skinned and
boned salmon.

variations

cheese soufflé

see base recipe page 89

cheese & shallot soufflé
Prepare the basic recipe, adding 2 finely chopped shallots, sautéed in a little butter until tender, to the sauce with the egg yolks.

mushroom & shallot soufflé
Prepare the basic recipe, omitting the cheese and mustard. Add 230 g (8 oz) finely chopped mushrooms, sautéed in a little butter with 2 finely chopped shallots until tender.

cheese & chive soufflé
Prepare the basic recipe, adding 3 tablespoons chopped chives to the sauce with the egg yolks.

smoked salmon soufflé
Prepare the basic recipe, omitting the cheese and mustard. Add 340 g (12 oz) very finely chopped smoked salmon to the sauce with the egg yolks.

spinach & shallot soufflé
Prepare the basic recipe, omitting the cheese and mustard. Add 110 g (4 oz) cooked, cooled and finely chopped spinach and 2 sautéed finely chopped shallots. Add both to the sauce with the egg yolks.

chicken satay with peanut sauce

see base recipe page 90

lamb satay with peanut sauce
Prepare the basic recipe, replacing the chicken with lean strips of lamb.

vegetarian satay with peanut sauce
Prepare the basic recipe, replacing the chicken with chunks of soy protein.

beef satay with peanut sauce
Prepare the basic recipe, replacing the chicken with strips of lean beef, such as filet.

vegetable skewers with peanut sauce
Prepare the basic recipe, replacing the chicken with chunks of prepared vegetables, such as courgettes, red and green peppers, red onion and aubergine.

variations

smoked mackerel pâté

see base recipe page 92

smoked mackerel pâté with green onions & dill
Prepare the basic recipe, adding 2 tablespoons finely chopped green onions and 2 teaspoons fresh dill to the food processor.

smoked salmon pâté
Prepare the basic recipe, replacing the mackerel with smoked salmon.

dairy-free smoked trout pâté
Prepare the basic recipe, replacing the mackerel with smoked trout and the cream cheese and soured cream with dairy-free cream cheese and mayonnaise.

smoked mackerel pâté in cucumbers
Prepare the basic recipe. Thinly peel 2 cucumbers, cut them both in half lengthwise and scoop out the seeds. Fill the hollow with pâté and serve chilled, sprinkled with a little paprika.

aubergine stuffed with crab

see base recipe page 93

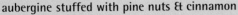

aubergine stuffed with pine nuts & cinnamon
Prepare the basic recipe, replacing the crab and paprika with 110 g (4 oz) pine nuts and 2 teaspoons ground cinnamon.

aubergine stuffed with celery & cheddar cheese
Prepare the basic recipe, replacing the crab with 170 g (6 oz) cooked chopped celery and 60 g (2 oz) shredded Cheddar cheese.

aubergine stuffed with chilli & beans
Prepare the basic recipe, replacing the crab with 170 g (6 oz) mixed cooked beans and 2 teaspoons finely chopped chilli pepper.

aubergine stuffed with cashews & chickpeas
Prepare the basic recipe, replacing the crab with 170 g (6 oz) cooked chickpeas and 60 g (2 oz) chopped cashews.

aubergine stuffed with quinoa & coconut
Prepare the basic recipe, replacing the crab with 230 g (8 oz) cooked quinoa and 30 g (1 oz) unsweetened shredded coconut.

bread & yeast

In this chapter you will find a diverse collection of rolls, bread, fruit breads and pizza dough all, of course, gluten-free. If you ever have any leftover homemade gluten-free bread, turn it into breadcrumbs in a food processor, and store in a sealed, labelled bag in your freezer for up to three months.

basic quick pizza dough

see variations page 129

This pizza dough tastes very authentic and is quick to prepare. It is a useful recipe too, if you are intolerant to yeast.

40 g (1½ oz) potato starch
40 g (1½ oz) sweet rice flour
100 g (3½ oz) white rice flour
1 tsp xantham gum

1 tsp baking powder
¼ tsp salt
1 tsp olive oil
120 ml (4 fl. oz) water

Preheat the oven to 200°C (400°F/Gas mark 6).

Place all the ingredients into a food processor and pulse until the mixture comes together in a soft dough. If the mixture looks too dry, add a little more water and if it looks too sticky, add a little more rice flour. The dough should be soft and pliable.

Transfer the dough to a lightly greased baking tray, sprinkle with rice flour and using your fingers, press into a round pizza crust about 18 cm (7 in) diameter. Bake in the oven for 5 minutes. Remove and spread with pizza sauce (page 112) and toppings and finish cooking.

Makes 1 pizza crust

pepperoni pizza made with yeast dough

see variations page 130

This dough is so good, you will hardly notice that it is not the usual pizza crust.

for the sauce
1 tbsp olive oil
1 small onion, finely chopped
1 500 g (16-oz) tin chopped
    tomatoes in juice
1 vegetable or chicken
    stock cube
2 tsp soya sauce
2 tsp Worcestershire sauce
1 tsp sugar
4 tbsp tomato paste
salt and freshly ground
    black pepper

for the yeast dough
1 tsp sugar
150 ml (5 fl. oz) lukewarm
    milk (45°C/110°F)
1 tbsp dry yeast
70 g (2½ oz) brown
    rice flour
50 g (1¾ oz)
    tapioca flour
50 g (1¾ oz) white rice flour,
    plus extra for sprinkling
pinch salt
2 tsp xantham gum

1½ tsp unflavoured
    gelatin powder
2 tsp dried mixed herbs
1 tsp olive oil
1 tsp cider vinegar

to finish the pizza
6 tbsp shredded
    Cheddar cheese
10 slices pepperoni
85 g (3 oz) mozzarella cheese,
    sliced
large handful freshly chopped
    basil leaves

To make the sauce, in a medium saucepan, heat the oil and sauté the onion until softened. Add chopped tomatoes, stock cube, soya sauce, Worcestershire sauce, sugar and tomato paste. Simmer until thickened. Season with salt and pepper.

Meanwhile, to make the dough, dissolve the sugar in the warm milk, sprinkle the yeast on top and leave for 10–15 minutes until frothy. Preheat the oven to 200°C (400°F/Gas mark 6).

In the bowl of a freestanding tabletop mixer and using the regular hook, not a dough hook, combine the flours, salt, xantham gum, gelatin powder and herbs on a low speed. Add the yeast liquid, oil and vinegar and mix to a soft dough. If the dough feels a little sticky, add more rice flour. If it feels too dry, add a little water.

Transfer the dough to a greased baking tray, sprinkle with rice flour and, using your fingers, press it into a round pizza base, about 25 cm (10 in) in diameter. Bake for 10 minutes. Remove from the oven and spread the crust with about 5 tablespoons of the tomato sauce, sprinkle with half the cheese and arrange pepperoni slices on top. Add slices of mozzarella, basil leaves and remaining Cheddar. Return to the oven for 10 minutes or until the crust is cooked through and the cheese has melted and is golden brown.

Makes 1 pizza

garlic & thyme focaccia

see variations page 131

Focaccia is an Italian flatbread, fast to make and just as quick to disappear.

butter, for greasing
cornmeal, for sprinkling
1 tsp sugar
120 ml (4 fl. oz) warm water (45°C/110°F)
1 envelope dry yeast
100 g (3½ oz) sorghum flour
70 g (2½ oz) tapioca flour
70 g (2½ oz) white rice flour
85 g (3 oz) potato starch
2 tsp xantham gum

1 tsp salt
1 large egg, room temperature, lightly beaten
4 tbsp olive oil, plus extra for drizzling
1 tbsp honey
1 tsp cider vinegar
2 cloves garlic, very finely chopped
2 tsp dried thyme
1 tsp coarse sea salt
1 clove garlic, finely chopped

Grease a 20-cm (9-in) cake tin with butter and sprinkle the base with cornmeal. Dissolve the sugar in the warm water and sprinkle the yeast on top. Leave until frothy, about 15 minutes.

In a large bowl, mix together the flours, potato starch, xantham gum and salt. Make a well in the centre and pour in the yeast liquid, egg, oil, honey, vinegar, garlic and thyme. Mix to a sticky dough and scoop it into the cake tin. Make a few indentations in the surface with your fingers, sprinkle with the sea salt and garlic and drizzle with a little olive oil. Leave, loosely covered, in a warm place for 30 minutes to rise.

Preheat the oven to 190°C (375°F/Gas mark 5). Bake the bread for 20–25 minutes or until golden and firm. Remove from the oven, allow to cool for a few minutes and transfer to cool on a wire rack.

Makes 8 wedges

soft dinner rolls

see variations page 132

Amazingly these rolls actually feel and taste like real bread! The dough is very soft, so they are formed into rolls rather than kneaded or rolled out.

50 g (1³/₄ oz) tapioca flour
70 g (2¹/₂ oz) white rice flour
170 g (6 oz) potato starch
60 g (2 oz) cornflour
1¹/₂ tsp salt
60 g (2 oz) fine cornmeal

60 g (2 oz) ground almonds
1 tsp sugar
2 tsp xantham gum
2 envelopes dry yeast
355 ml (12 fl. oz) warm water (45°C/110°F)
2 tbsp olive oil

Preheat the oven to 200°C (400°F/Gas mark 6). Grease and flour a baking tray. In a food processor, sift together the flours, potato starch, cornflour and salt. Add the cornmeal, ground almonds, sugar, xantham gum and yeast. Pulse again briefly to mix. In a large measuring jug, whisk together the warm water and the olive oil. Pour two-thirds of the liquid into the food processor and pulse 3–4 times. Add half the remaining liquid and pulse again briefly. Now add the liquid 1 tablespoon at a time until the mixture is a dropping consistency. It should hold its shape well and should just fall off a spoon.

Place large spoonfuls of the mixture onto the baking tray, form the dough into the shape of rolls and smooth the surface with the back of a wet spoon. Bake in the oven for 15–20 minutes until risen, golden brown and cooked through. Cool on a wire rack until just warm. Do not cut when hot or the rolls will collapse. Best served warm. The rolls will keep for 24 hours in an airtight container or can be immediately frozen for up to 1 month.

Makes 6–7

irish soda bread

see variations page 133

This bread has the advantage of being made very quickly. It is easy to throw together just before lunch, perhaps to go with soup or a salad. As soon as the buttermilk mixes with the bicarbonate of soda, it will start to react, so work quickly, but do not overwork the dough.

450 g (1 lb) GF plain flour mix
  (page 16)
2 tsp xantham gum

1 tsp salt
1 tsp bicarbonate of soda
240 ml (8 fl. oz) plus 2 tbsp buttermilk

Preheat the oven to 175°C (350°F/Gas mark 4) and lightly grease a baking tray.

In a large bowl, mix together the flour mix, xantham gum, salt and bicarbonate of soda. Make a well in the centre and pour in the buttermilk, mixing lightly with a fork to make a soft dough. If it feels too dry, add a little more buttermilk or if it seems too sticky, add a little more flour mix. Turn the dough out onto a lightly floured work surface and knead just a couple of times to form it into a thick round.

Transfer to the baking tray and make a deep cut in the shape of a cross on top of the dough. This helps the bread rise. Bake in the oven for 35–40 minutes or until well risen and light golden in colour. Cool on a wire rack before slicing or cutting.

Makes 1 loaf

spicy mexican cornbread

see variations page 134

This spicy cornbread is really colourful and extremely good with a chilli dish. Use as much mild or hot chilli as you like.

280 g (10 oz) cornmeal
1 tsp salt
1 tsp baking powder
1 tsp bicarbonate of soda
110 g (4 oz) finely chopped green
    onions, green part only
110 g (4 oz) finely shredded Cheddar cheese

1 or 2 red chillies, mild or hot, finely chopped
2 eggs
470 ml (16 fl. oz) buttermilk
1 400-g (14-oz) tin creamed corn
60 ml (2 fl. oz) olive oil

Preheat the oven to 190°C (375°F/Gas mark 5) and grease a 22x33-cm (9x13-in) loaf tin.

In a large bowl, mix the cornmeal with the salt, baking powder, bicarbonate of soda, spring onions, cheese and chillies. In another bowl, whisk the eggs with the buttermilk, creamed corn and olive oil. Make a well in the centre of the cornmeal mix and quickly pour in the egg and buttermilk mixture. Stir lightly until just combined, pour into the loaf tin and bake in the oven for about 25 minutes or until golden brown and cooked through. Cool in the tin for 10 minutes, then turn out to cool on a wire rack.

Makes 1 loaf

mixed dried fruit bread

see variations page 135

This delicious recipe is excellent as fruit cake as well as fruit bread.

85 g (3 oz) chopped dried apples
40 g (1½ oz) chopped dried apricots
40 g (1½ oz) chopped dried dates
40 g (1½ oz) dried cranberries
85 g (3 oz) mixed dried fruit
1 tbsp treacle
120 ml (4 fl. oz) apple juice, heated until hot
    but not boiling
30 g (1 oz) chopped pecans
35 g (1¼ oz) white rice flour
30 g (1 oz) cornflour

30 g (1 oz) ground almonds
40 g (1½ oz) potato starch
1 tsp xantham gum
1 tsp baking powder
2 tsp ground cinnamon
1 tsp ground nutmeg
60 g (2 oz) butter, softened
140 g (5 oz) brown sugar
2 large eggs
zest of 1 orange and 1 lemon
110 g (4 oz) apple sauce

In a large bowl, place all the dried fruit and treacle. Pour in the apple juice, cover and soak at room temperature overnight. The following day, preheat the oven to 175°C (350°F/Gas mark 4). Grease two 900-g (2-lb) loaf tins. In a large bowl, mix together the pecans, flour, cornflour, ground almonds, potato starch, xantham gum, baking powder, cinnamon and nutmeg.

In another bowl, cream the butter and brown sugar together. Add the eggs, one at a time, beating well after each one. Add the flour mixture, orange and lemon zest, apple sauce and fruit mixture. Stir until just combined. Divide the mixture between the loaf tins and bake for about 1 hour or until a cocktail stick inserted in the centre of each loaf comes out clean. Cool in the tin for 10 minutes, then turn out to cool completely on a wire rack.
Makes 2 loaves

banana, date & walnut bread

see variations page 136

The banana and honey in this bread helps keep it moist and the flavour is enhanced with the addition of dates and walnuts.

6 tbsp softened unsalted butter, plus extra
   for greasing
110 g (4 oz) caster sugar
255 g (9 oz) GF plain flour mix
   (page 16)
$^1/_2$ tsp salt
2 tsp xantham gum

2 tsp baking powder
$^1/_4$ tsp bicarbonate of soda
3 medium-size bananas (2 very ripe)
60 ml (2 fl. oz) buttermilk
2 large eggs, beaten
60 g (2 oz) finely chopped dried dates
60 g (2 oz) finely chopped walnuts

Preheat the oven to 175°C (350°F/Gas mark 4). Butter a 450-g (1-lb) loaf tin and dust with flour. In a large bowl, beat the butter and sugar together until creamy. In a separate bowl, combine the dry ingredients. In yet another bowl, mash the 2 very ripe bananas with the buttermilk.

Add the beaten eggs gradually to the creamed butter and sugar. Add the mashed bananas and the dry ingredients and mix lightly until combined. Do not over mix. Slice the third banana and add it to the batter with the dates and walnuts, stirring lightly, until just combined. Pour the batter into the loaf tin and bake in the middle of the oven for about 40 minutes or until a cocktail stick inserted into the centre comes out clean. Allow to cool in the tin for 10 minutes, then turn out and cool completely on a wire rack before slicing.

Makes 1 loaf

seeded sandwich loaf

see variations page 137

This is a tasty bread, full of seeds, with lots of texture to add interest to a sandwich.

1 tsp sugar
355 ml (12 fl. oz) warm water (45°C/110°F)
1 envelope dry yeast
340 g (12 oz) GF plain flour mix
    (page 16)
2 tsp xantham gum
1 tsp salt

3 eggs
1 tbsp honey
1 tbsp olive oil
1 tsp cider vinegar
3 tbsp mixed seeds (e.g., poppy, millet,
    flax, sesame)

Dissolve the sugar in the warm water, sprinkle the yeast on top and leave until frothy, about 10–15 minutes. In a large bowl, combine the plain flour mix with the xantham gum and salt. In another bowl, whisk the eggs, honey, oil and vinegar until frothy. Make a well in the centre of the flour and pour in the yeast liquid, the egg mixture and 2 tablespoons seeds. Mix with an electric mixer for 4 minutes. Scoop into the loaf tin, cover loosely and leave to rise until the dough is 2.5 cm (1 in) above the edge of the tin.

Preheat the oven to 190°C (375°F/Gas mark 5). Sprinkle the top of the loaf with the remaining seeds and bake for 50–60 minutes. Remove from the oven and allow to cool in the tin for 10 minutes, then turn out and allow to cool completely on a wire rack before slicing.

Makes 1 loaf

buttermilk biscuits

see variations page 138

These biscuits are fluffy and light and so versatile.

110 g (4 oz) brown rice flour
85 g (3 oz) cornflour
40 g (1½ oz) potato starch
70 g (2½ oz) white rice flour,
    plus more for sprinkling
1 tsp xantham gum
4 tsp baking powder
1 tsp bicarbonate of soda

1 tsp cream of tartar
1 tsp salt
5 tbsp (2½ oz) unsalted butter (placed in
    freezer for 2 hours)
240 ml (8 fl. oz) buttermilk
1 egg
1 egg mixed with 1 tbsp water, for glazing

Preheat the oven to 220°C (425°F/Gas mark 7). Line 2 baking trays with parchment paper and grease with a little vegetable oil. In a large bowl, mix together the dry ingredients until well combined. Remove butter from the freezer and grate directly into the flour mixture. Cut in with a pastry cutter or your fingers until the mixture resembles fine breadcrumbs. In a small bowl, whisk buttermilk and egg together. Make a well in the centre of the flour and pour in the buttermilk and egg, stirring lightly with a fork until just combined. Place a sheet of clingfilm on the work surface, place the dough on top and another layer of clingfilm on top of the dough. With a rolling pin, gently roll the dough, through the clingfilm, to a thickness of 2 cm (¾ in) and remove the top layer of clingfilm. Sprinkle the dough with a little white rice flour. Oil a 6-cm (2¼-in) pastry cutter and cut out as many biscuits as you can, re-rolling the dough as necessary. Transfer the biscuits to the baking trays and brush with a little egg glaze. Place in the oven, immediately turn the heat down to 200°C (400°F/Gas mark 6) and bake the biscuits for 15–18 minutes. Serve warm or freeze as soon as they have cooled, for up to 1 month.
Makes about 12 biscuits

cherry brioche

see variations page 139

This butter-rich French-style loaf is ideal for breakfast. It is also excellent for making French toast.

1 tsp sugar
120 ml (4 fl. oz) warm milk (45°C/110°F)
1 envelope dry yeast
110 g (4 oz) cornflour
50 g (1¾ oz) white rice flour
40 g (1½ oz) tapioca flour
40 g (1½ oz) potato starch
2 tsp xantham gum

1 tsp salt
5 tbsp butter (2½ oz), melted and cooled
2 eggs
2 tbsp honey
2 tsp vanilla extract
140 g (5 oz) dried cherries
1 tbsp raw cane sugar

Dissolve the sugar in the warm milk, sprinkle the yeast on top and leave for 10–15 minutes until frothy. In a large bowl, mix together the cornflour, flours, potato starch, xantham gum, salt and sugar. In another bowl, whisk together the melted butter, eggs, honey and vanilla extract. Make a well in the centre of the flour mix and pour in the milk liquid and yeast liquid. Beat well until combined. Stir in the dried cherries. Put the dough in an oiled bowl, turn it around, cover with clingfilm and leave at room temperature to rise, for an hour. Grease a 23x13-cm (9x5-in) loaf tin. Transfer the dough to the loaf tin and carefully smooth the top. Sprinkle with raw cane sugar, cover loosely and leave to rise again for an hour.

Preheat the oven to 200°C (400°F/Gas mark 6). Bake the loaf for 25–30 minutes or until well risen and golden brown. Allow to cool for 10 minutes before turning out to cool completely on a wire rack before slicing.

Makes 1 loaf

variations

basic quick pizza dough

see base recipe page 111

potato pizza dough
Prepare the basic recipe, omitting the xantham gum and the water.
Replace with extra baking powder and olive oil (2 teaspoons of each).
Also add 230 g (8 oz) mashed potato to the processor.

butternut squash pizza dough
Instead of the basic recipe, in a food processor, combine 230 g (8 oz)
butternut squash purée, 60 g (1²/₃ oz) coconut flour, 130 g (4½ oz) brown
rice flour, 1 tablespoon olive oil, 1 tablespoon baking powder, 1 teaspoon
dried Italian herbs and a pinch of salt. Roll out to 26-cm (10-in) pizza
base. Bake for 10 minutes before adding toppings.

biscuit crust pizza dough
Instead of the basic recipe, combine 130 g (4½ oz) brown rice flour, 170 g
(6 oz) potato starch, 1 teaspoon xantham gum, 1 tablespoon baking
powder, 1 teaspoon cream of tartar, ¾ teaspoon each of bicarbonate of
soda and salt and 1 teaspoon sugar. Rub in 60 g (2 oz) butter, add 1 egg,
180 ml (6 fl. oz) milk and mix to a soft dough. Roll out to 26-cm (10-in)
pizza base.

variations

pepperoni pizza made with yeast dough

see base recipe page 112

chargrilled chicken, onion & barbecue sauce pizza
Prepare the basic recipe, replacing the tomato sauce with barbecue sauce and the pepperoni with 60 g (2 oz) chopped chargrilled chicken and 2 tablespoons cooked chopped onion.

goat's cheese, caramelised onion & cherry tomato pizza
Prepare the basic recipe, replacing the pepperoni and both cheeses with 85 g (3 oz) diced goat's cheese, 70 g (2½ oz) caramelised onion (page 101) and 8 cherry tomatoes.

oven-roasted mediterranean vegetable pizza
Prepare the basic recipe, replacing the pepperoni with a selection of chopped Mediterranean vegetables, such as courgettes, peppers, aubergine and tomatoes, roasted for 30 minutes in a medium oven, drizzled with olive oil.

tuna, anchovies, tomato & olive pizza
Prepare the basic recipe, replacing the pepperoni with 110 g (4 oz) drained tinned tuna chunks, 40 g (1½ oz) drained tinned anchovies, 2 quartered tomatoes and a scattering of pitted black olives.

garlic & thyme focaccia

see base recipe page 115

garlic, onion & rosemary focaccia
Prepare the basic recipe, omitting the thyme. Add 1 very finely chopped small onion, sautéed in a little oil and cooled and 2 teaspoons dried rosemary to the mix.

garlic, tomato & oregano focaccia
Prepare the basic recipe, replacing the thyme with 2 teaspoons dried oregano. Add several halved cherry tomatoes to the top of the bread before baking.

garlic, pepper & coriander focaccia
Prepare the basic recipe, replacing the thyme with 1 tablespoon freshly chopped coriander and 1 very finely chopped pepper.

garlic, courgette & basil focaccia
Prepare the basic recipe, replacing the thyme with 1 tablespoon freshly chopped basil. Add a few pieces of chopped courgette to the top of the bread before baking.

garlic, parmesan & chive focaccia
Prepare the basic recipe, replacing the thyme with 1 tablespoon freshly chopped chives. Add 30 g (1 oz) freshly grated Parmesan cheese to the mix.

variations

soft dinner rolls

see base recipe page 116

soft hot dog rolls
Prepare the basic recipe, forming the dough into the shape of hot dog buns.

soft seeded dinner rolls with Parmesan
Prepare the basic recipe, adding 1 tablespoon poppy seeds to the processor with the liquid. Just before baking, sprinkle each roll with a little finely grated Parmesan cheese.

hamburger buns
Prepare the basic recipe, forming the dough into flatter buns. Just before baking, sprinkle each bun with 1 teaspoon sesame seeds.

soft garlic dinner rolls topped with sunflower seeds
Prepare the basic recipe. Add 1 minced garlic clove to the processor with the liquid. Just before baking, sprinkle each roll with 1 teaspoon sunflower seeds.

variations

irish soda bread

see base recipe page 119

cheese & mustard soda bread
Prepare the basic recipe, adding 40 g (1½ oz) shredded Cheddar cheese and
2 teaspoons dry mustard to the mixture.

tomato basil soda bread
Prepare the basic recipe, adding 2 tablespoons finely chopped sun-dried
tomatoes and 1 tablespoon freshly chopped basil.

garlic & rosemary soda bread
Prepare the basic recipe, adding 1 minced clove garlic and
1 tablespoon dried rosemary.

oregano & poppy seed soda bread
Prepare the basic recipe, adding 1 tablespoon dried oregano and 1 tablespoon
poppy seeds.

italian fresh herb soda bread
Prepare the basic recipe, adding 2 tablespoons each chopped fresh parsley and
oregano, and 1 tablespoon chopped fresh rosemary.

variations

spicy mexican cornbread

see base recipe page 120

spicy mexican cornbread with coriander
Prepare the basic recipe, adding 2 tablespoons freshly chopped coriander with the onions.

spicy mexican cornbread with cardamom
Prepare the basic recipe, adding 1 teaspoon cardamom seeds with the onions.

spicy mexican cornbread with sun-dried tomatoes
Prepare the basic recipe, adding 60 g (2 oz) finely chopped sun-dried tomatoes and 2 tablespoons freshly chopped basil with the onions.

spicy mexican cornbread with pumpkin seeds
Prepare the basic recipe, adding 2 tablespoons pumpkin seeds with the onions.

spicy mexican cornbread with peppers
Prepare the basic recipe, adding 3 tablespoons very finely chopped red pepper with the onions.

variations

mixed dried fruit bread

see base recipe page 123

fruit bread with cherries & brandy
Prepare the basic recipe, replacing the apple and apple juice with glacé cherries and brandy.

mixed dried fruit bread with figs & walnuts
Prepare the basic recipe, replacing the apple and pecans with chopped dried figs and walnuts.

fruit bread with glacé fruit topping
Prepare the basic recipe and add a glacé fruit topping to the cooled cake. Heat gently 4 tablespoons apricot preserve with 2 tablespoons water, then pass through a sieve into a small bowl. Brush the top of the cake with a little apricot glaze, arrange a selection of glacé fruit on top and brush with more glaze. Tie a wide ribbon around the cake.

mixed dried fruit bread with mixed peel
Prepare the basic recipe, adding 40 g (1¹/₂ oz) mixed dried peel to the mixture with the dried fruit.

variations

banana, date & walnut bread

see base recipe page 124

banana cranberry bread
Prepare the basic recipe, replacing the dates and walnuts with
110 g (4 oz) chopped dried cranberries.

banana, fig & pecan bread
Prepare the basic recipe, replacing the dates with dried figs and the
walnuts with pecans.

banana, apple & ginger bread
Prepare the basic recipe, omitting the dates and walnuts. Replace
with 110 g (4 oz) finely chopped dried apples and 2 teaspoons
ground ginger.

banana, cherry & coconut bread
Prepare the basic recipe, omitting the dates and walnuts.
Replace with 60 g (2 oz) finely chopped dried cherries
and 30 g (1 oz) unsweetened flaked coconut.

seeded sandwich loaf

see base recipe page 126

oaty sandwich loaf
Prepare the basic recipe, omitting the seeds. Add 30 g (1 oz) rolled oats to the flour mix. Sprinkle the top of the loaf with 1 tablespoon rolled oats.

seeded parmesan sandwich loaf
Prepare the basic recipe, adding 2 tablespoons freshly grated Parmesan to the flour mix.

onion & dill sandwich loaf
Prepare the basic recipe, replacing the seeds in the flour mix with 2 tablespoons dried onion flakes and 2 teaspoons dried dill. Sprinkle the top of the loaf with 1 tablespoon dried onions.

garlic & basil sandwich loaf
Prepare the basic recipe, omitting the poppy seeds. Replace with 1 minced garlic clove and 2 teaspoons dried basil, added to the flour mix. Sprinkle the top of the loaf with 1 tablespoon dried basil.

chilli & coriander sandwich loaf
Prepare the basic recipe, omitting the poppy seeds. Replace with 1 seeded and finely chopped mild red chilli and 1 tablespoon freshly chopped coriander, added to the flour mix. Sprinkle the top of the loaf with 2 teaspoons dried red chilli flakes.

variations

buttermilk biscuits

see base recipe page 127

parmesan biscuits
Prepare the basic recipe, adding 30 g (1 oz) freshly grated Parmesan to the mixture.

sausage & mustard biscuits
Prepare the basic recipe, adding 60 g (2 oz) finely chopped cooked sausage and 2 teaspoons Dijon mustard to the mixture.

sage & onion biscuits
Prepare the basic recipe, adding 2 teaspoons dried sage and 1 tablespoon dried onion flakes to the mixture.

bacon & sun-dried tomato biscuits
Prepare the basic recipe, adding 2 strips finely chopped crisply cooked bacon and 2 tablespoons finely chopped sun-dried tomatoes to the mixture.

variations

cherry brioche

see base recipe page 128

orange & almond brioche
Prepare the basic recipe, omitting the tapioca flour, vanilla and cherries.
Replace with 40 g (1½ oz) ground almonds, almond extract and the
zest of 1 orange.

apricot & cinnamon brioche
Prepare the basic recipe, replacing the cherries with finely chopped dried apricots
and the vanilla with almond extract. Add 1 teaspoon ground cinnamon.

golden raisin & lemon brioche
Prepare the basic recipe, replacing the cherries with golden raisins and adding
the zest of 1 lemon.

chocolate chip brioche
Prepare the basic recipe, replacing the cherries with plain chocolate chips.

ginger & apple brioche
Prepare the basic recipe, replacing the cherries with finely chopped dried apples
and adding 1 teaspoon ground ginger.

mains

From casual weeknight family meals to elegant

dinner party dishes, this chapter will provide

inspiration for all your day-to-day needs.

beef in red wine sauce with mushrooms

see variations page 176

A warming rich beef stew, full of vegetables and hearty enough to satisfy on the coldest winter night.

35 g (1¼ oz) white rice flour
30 g (1 oz) cornflour
salt and freshly ground black pepper
900 g (2 lbs) lean beef, trimmed and cubed
2 tbsp olive oil, plus extra if necessary
6 strips bacon, chopped
1 large onion, finely chopped
3 cloves garlic, crushed

230 g (8 oz) sliced mushrooms
2 carrots, sliced
3 tbsp tomato paste
1 tbsp dried mixed Italian herbs
240 ml (8 fl. oz) good-quality beef stock
1 beef stock cube
240 ml (8 fl. oz) red wine
3 tbsp freshly chopped parsley

Preheat the oven to 160°C (325°F/Gas mark 3). Mix rice flour and cornflour on a plate and add salt and pepper. Roll the beef in the flour until well coated. In a large frying pan, heat the oil. Brown the beef in batches and transfer to a large ovenproof casserole dish. Add the bacon and fry over a medium heat for 5 minutes until crisp, then add to the beef. Pour away any excess bacon fat and add the onion and garlic to the frying pan. Fry for 5 minutes until softened, then add the mushrooms, carrots, tomato paste, herbs, stock, stock cube and red wine to the frying pan. Heat, stirring, to deglaze the tin. Transfer to the casserole dish, cover and cook in the oven for 2½–3 hours, until the beef is tender, checking occasionally and adding extra water or stock if it becomes a too dry. Remove from the oven, taste and adjust the seasoning if necessary. Stir in the parsley and serve immediately.

Serves 6

savoury beef tarts with crispy potato topping

see variations page 177

Meat and a rich gravy in a pastry crust with mashed potatoes, crisped and browned under the grill.

450 g (1 lb) lean ground beef
1 medium onion, finely chopped
1 clove garlic, crushed
355 ml (12 fl. oz) good-quality beef stock
1 beef stock cube
2 tsp dried Italian herbs
2 tsp Worcestershire sauce
2 tsp soya sauce
1 tbsp tomato ketchup
1 large carrot, finely chopped

60 g (2 oz) frozen peas
salt and freshly ground black pepper
2 tsp cornflour
2 tbsp cold water
450 g (1 lb) potatoes, peeled and cut into
    chunks
1 tbsp (½ oz) butter
4 part-baked 13-cm (5-in) GF pastry crusts
    (page 17)

In a large saucepan, fry the beef for 10 minutes, stirring continuously, until lightly browned. Add the onion and garlic and continue to cook for 10 minutes, until the onion has softened. Add the stock, stock cube, herbs, Worcestershire and soya sauce, ketchup and carrot. Stir to combine. Cover and simmer gently for about 30 minutes. Add the peas, simmer for 5 minutes and season to taste with a little salt and plenty of pepper. In a small bowl, mix the cornflour with the cold water, then stir the mixture into the meat and gravy.

Continue to stir until the gravy has returned to a simmer and has thickened. Transfer to a bowl, cover and set aside to cool.

Wash the saucepan and fill it three-quarters full with cold water. Add the potatoes and boil them for about 20 minutes until tender. Drain, tip back into the saucepan and mash lightly with a potato masher. Add the butter and season with salt and pepper. Set aside.

Preheat the oven to 175°C (350°F/Gas mark 4). Spoon the cooled meat and gravy into the pastry crusts to a level just below the edge of the crust. Spoon the potatoes on top. Place the filled crusts on a baking tray and transfer to the oven. Bake for about 30 minutes until piping hot. If the tops are not browned enough already, grill for 2–3 minutes under the grill to crisp. Serve immediately.

Serves 4

breaded fried chicken with parmesan

see variations page 178

If you thought breaded fried chicken was off your menu, think again.

2 tbsp canola oil, plus extra for greasing
4 boneless, skinless chicken breasts
70 g (2½ oz) white rice flour
1–2 eggs, beaten
230 g (8 oz) GF breadcrumbs

40 g (1½ oz) finely shredded
    Parmesan cheese
1 tsp Cajun seasoning
salt and freshly ground black pepper
watercress and lemon wedges, to serve

Grease a baking tray with a little oil.

Lay each chicken breast in turn on a sheet of parchment paper. Cover with another sheet of parchment paper and using a meat mallet or rolling pin, beat each breast until it is much thinner. Place the rice flour on a plate, the beaten egg on a second and the breadcrumbs on a third. Add the Parmesan cheese, Cajun seasoning and salt and pepper to the breadcrumbs. Dredge each piece of chicken in flour, roll in the egg and cover in breadcrumbs. Place on a plate, cover and chill for 30 minutes. Preheat the oven to 190°C (375°F/Gas mark 5).

In a large frying pan, heat 2 tablespoons canola oil. When it is hot, but not smoking, fry each chicken breast for 3–4 minutes each side, until golden brown. Add more oil, if needed. Transfer the chicken to the greased baking tray and bake for about 30 minutes. Serve immediately, garnished with watercress and a lemon wedge.

Serves 4

steak & onion pie

see variations page 179

Start this delectable steak and onion dish either first thing in the morning or even better, the day before, to allow the flavours to develop and mature.

700 g (1½ lbs) lean steak, trimmed and cut into
    2.5-cm (1-in) cubes
35 g (1¼ oz) white rice flour
salt and freshly ground black pepper
2 tbsp canola oil, plus extra if needed
2 large onions, roughly chopped
2 cloves garlic, crushed
700 ml (24 fl. oz) good-quality beef stock

2 beef stock cubes
2 tbsp tomato paste
1 tsp dried mixed Italian herbs
2 tsp freshly chopped parsley
GF shortcrust pastry (page 19)
1 egg, lightly beaten

Preheat the oven to 150°C (300°F/Gas mark 2). Put the rice flour on a large plate, season with salt and pepper, add the beef and turn it around in the flour to coat it all over. In a large frying pan, heat the oil and when it is hot, but not smoking, add the beef. Fry for a few minutes, turning it around with a spatula, until it is browned all over. You may need to do this in batches. Transfer to an ovenproof casserole and set aside.

Add a little more oil to the frying pan if needed, add the onions and garlic and cook for about 5 minutes over a medium heat, until softened. Add the stock and stir to deglaze. Add the stock cubes, tomato paste and herbs, then transfer to the casserole. Cover and bake in the oven for about 3–4 hours or until the beef is meltingly tender. Remove from the oven and allow to cool, preferably overnight, if you have time.

Preheat the oven to 200°C (400°F/Gas mark 6). Place the beef and onions in a deep 23-cm (9-in) oval pie dish. Roll out the pastry until it is 2.5–5cm (1–2 in) larger than the pie dish. Dampen the edge of the pie dish with water. Cut a strip off the pastry to line the edge of the dish. Brush the pastry edges with water so they will stick. Place the pastry on top, sealing it at the edges. Brush with a little beaten egg and decorate the pie with pastry trimmings cut into leaf shapes.

With the tip of a knife, cut a small hole in the middle of the pie to let the steam out. Bake for about 30 minutes or until the pastry is cooked and golden brown. Serve immediately.
Serves 4

beef cannelloni with tomato sauce

see variations page 180

This is a delicious cheese and beef mixture, rolled up in gluten-free lasagna noodles, and covered with a tasty tomato sauce. They are baked in the oven in one dish or in individual portions.

12 GF lasagna noodles
500 g (18 oz) lean ground beef
1 large onion, finely chopped
2 cloves garlic, crushed
40 g (1½ oz) dry GF breadcrumbs
2 tbsp chopped parsley
1 tsp dried oregano
60 ml (2 fl. oz) dry white wine
1 egg

60 g (2 oz) grated fontina cheese
salt and freshly ground black pepper
butter for greasing
2 tbsp freshly grated Parmesan cheese, to serve

for the tomato sauce
1 tbsp olive oil
1 medium onion, finely chopped
2 cloves garlic, crushed

1 425-g (15-oz) tin chopped tomatoes in juice
1 tsp fresh thyme leaves
1 tsp fresh oregano
85 g (3 oz) freshly grated Parmesan cheese
4 tbsp tomato paste
1 tsp soya sauce
1 tsp Worcestershire sauce
1 chicken stock cube
1 tsp sugar
salt and freshly ground black pepper

Grease a large shallow baking dish (or individual dishes). In a large saucepan three-quarters full of boiling water, cook the noodles as directed on the packet, stirring with a wooden spoon to prevent them sticking together. You may need to do this in batches. Drain and rinse with cold water and lay on a clean kitchen towel to dry. In a large saucepan, cook the beef for 10 minutes, until browned. Drain off the fat. Place the beef back in the pan, add the onion and garlic and cook over low heat for 15 minutes until softened. Allow to cool.

In a large bowl, mix the beef with the breadcrumbs and herbs. Add the wine, egg, fontina cheese, salt and pepper. Set aside. Preheat the oven to 175°C (350°F/Gas mark 4).

Make the tomato sauce. In a large saucepan, heat the oil and cook the onion and garlic until softened. Add the tomatoes, herbs, Parmesan cheese, tomato paste, soya sauce, Worcestershire sauce, stock cube and sugar. Simmer for 15 minutes. Season with salt and pepper to taste and set aside. Place 2–3 tablespoons filling on each lasagna noodle and roll up. In a large buttered serving dish, place 3 tablespoons tomato sauce. Place each cannelloni roll, seam-side down and side by side, on top. Cover with the rest of the tomato sauce, cover with buttered aluminium foil and bake for about 30 minutes. Sprinkle with Parmesan, to serve.

Serves 4

roast rack of lamb with gremolata & asparagus

see variations page 181

Gremolata is a wonderfully fragrant Italian garnish of parsley, lemon and garlic. Superb for a dinner party, elegant and sophisticated, this dish will wow your guests.

for the gremolata
4 tbsp freshly chopped parsley
finely shredded rind of 2 lemons
2–3 cloves garlic, finely chopped

10–12 bone rack of lamb
salt and freshly ground black pepper
2 tbsp vegetable oil
340 g (12 oz) asparagus spears
few fresh spinach leaves,
    and aïoli, to serve

In a small bowl, mix together the ingredients for the gremolata and set aside. Pre-heat the oven to 200°C (400°F/Gas mark 6). Trim the excess fat from the rack of lamb, cut into two racks and season well with salt and freshly ground black pepper. In a large oven-proof frying pan, heat the oil and when it is hot but not smoking, add the lamb and brown it for just 2 minutes each side. Transfer the frying pan to the oven and roast the lamb for about 20–25 minutes until it is cooked, but still a little pink in the centre. Remove the lamb from the oven and leave to rest for 10 minutes.

Meanwhile, blanche the asparagus in boiling salted water for 5 minutes. Drain and set aside. Slice the lamb into cutlets, sprinkle with gremolata, add the asparagus spears and serve each portion garnished with a little aïoli (page 183) and a few fresh spinach leaves.

Serves 4

slow-roasted lamb shoulder

see variations page 182

This rustic oven-roasted lamb, fragrant with the aroma of garlic and rosemary, will be so tender, the meat will just fall off the bone. Serve with a rich gravy.

1 shoulder of lamb, about 900 g (2 lbs) in
   weight, bone in
2 tbsp olive oil
salt and freshly ground black pepper
1 onion, roughly chopped
1 carrot, cut into small cubes
2 celery stalks, sliced
6 sprigs fresh rosemary
1 whole bulb garlic, unpeeled, separated
   into cloves

2 sage leaves, finely chopped
700 ml (24 fl. oz) white wine
470 ml (16 fl. oz) good-quality lamb
   or chicken stock
1 lamb or chicken stock cube
1 tbsp tomato paste
1 tbsp redcurrant jam
1 tbsp Worcestershire sauce
1 tbsp soya sauce
1 tbsp cornflour

Preheat the oven to 220°C (425°F/Gas mark 7). Lightly score the fat of the lamb with a sharp knife. Rub with olive oil, salt and freshly ground black pepper all over. Place the onion, carrot, celery, half the rosemary and half the garlic cloves in the base of a roasting tin. Sit the lamb on top and sprinkle with the sage leaves. Pour the wine around the lamb and vegetables, cover with a double layer of foil and seal tightly. Place into the oven, immediately turn the heat down to 150°C (300°F/Gas mark 2) and roast for 4 hours.

At the end of cooking time, remove the lamb from the oven and transfer it to a chopping board. Cover loosely with foil and allow to rest for 15 minutes.

Carefully pour off most of the fat from the juices and vegetables in the roasting tin, add 240 ml (8 fl. oz) water to the tin and place it on a medium heat on the stovetop. Bring to the boil, stirring to deglaze the tin. Strain the gravy into a medium saucepan and retrieve 5 of the garlic cloves. Mash them, discarding the skins and add to the gravy. Add the stock, stock cube, tomato paste, jam, Worcestershire and soya sauces and stir to combine. Add the cornflour, mixed with a little water to make a paste and stirring until thickened. Taste, and adjust seasoning if necessary. Pull lamb apart with forks and serve with the gravy.

Serves 6

jerk chicken with mango salsa

see variations page 183

You can make this chicken as spicy as you like and the mango salsa complements the flavour beautifully.

for the mango salsa
170 g (6 oz) diced ripe mango
110 g (4 oz) finely chopped red onion
110 g (4 oz) chopped tomatoes
2 tbsp freshly chopped coriander
1 red chilli, seeded and finely chopped
1 tbsp lime juice
salt and freshly ground black pepper

for the chicken
4 boneless, skinless chicken breasts
jerk seasoning
salt and freshly ground black pepper
2 tbsp canola oil

To make the salsa, in a medium bowl, mix together the diced mango, red onion, chopped tomatoes, chopped coriander, red chilli and lime juice. Season to taste with salt and pepper. Cover and chill until needed.

Cut the chicken breasts lengthwise in half to make 2 thinner escalopes. Thoroughly coat each one with jerk seasoning, salt and pepper. In a large frying pan, heat the canola oil and sauté the chicken escalopes for 4–5 minutes on each side over a high heat. Alternatively grill outside on the barbecue. Serve hot, with the mango salsa.

Serves 4

chicken korma

see variations page 184

A korma is a mild and creamy curry containing coconut milk and ground almonds, which give a lovely texture to the dish. Serve with pilau rice (page 221) and fragrant potato and cauliflower bhuna (page 207) for a curry feast.

3 tbsp canola oil
1 tbsp (1/2 oz) butter
4 skinless and boneless chicken fillets, cut into
    2.5-cm (1-in) cubes
1 large onion, roughly chopped
2 cloves garlic, crushed
1 mild green chilli, seeded and finely chopped
1 2.5-cm (1-in) piece fresh root ginger, peeled
    and shredded

1/2 tsp ground turmeric
1 tsp ground cumin
1 tsp ground coriander
1 400-g (14-oz) tin coconut milk
110 g (4 oz) ground almonds
120 ml (4 fl. oz) good-quality chicken stock
1 chicken stock cube
salt and freshly ground black pepper
sliced almonds, to serve

In a large frying pan, heat 2 tablespoons oil and the butter and when it is hot, but not smoking, add the chicken and fry over a high heat for about 7 minutes. Turn the chicken over with a spatula until nicely browned all over. Transfer with a slotted spoon to a plate and set aside.

Add the remaining oil to the frying pan and cook the onion and garlic over a medium heat for about 10 minutes, until soft and golden. Add the chilli, root ginger, turmeric, cumin and coriander and cook for 2 minutes. Add the coconut milk, ground almonds, chicken stock, stock cube, salt and pepper, stirring continuously. Return the chicken to the frying pan, cover and simmer over a gentle heat for 10 minutes. Remove the cover and cook for a further 10 minutes, until the sauce has thickened. Serve sprinkled with sliced almonds.
Serves 4

chicken enchiladas

see variations page 185

Tortillas made with corn are readily available from your local supermarket and make wonderful enchiladas. Satisfying and very filling, they are sure to be a hit.

for the salsa de jitomate
2 tbsp canola oil
1 large onion, finely sliced
1 clove garlic, crushed
3 400-g (14-oz) tins chopped
    tomatoes in juice
110 g (4 oz) tomato paste
2 green chillies, finely
    chopped
1 chicken stock cube
2 tsp sugar

2 tbsp chopped coriander
salt and freshly ground
    black pepper

for the enchiladas
2–4 tbsp canola oil
1 large onion, finely sliced
1 red pepper, seeded
    and sliced

4 skinless and boneless
    chicken breasts, sliced
    on the diagonal into
    thin strips
1 400-g (14-oz) tin whole
    kernel corn, drained
18 corn tortillas
340 g (12 oz) finely shredded
    Cheddar cheese
soured cream and lime
    wedges, to serve

Preheat the oven to 150°C (300°F/Gas mark 2). Make the salsa de jitomate. In a large saucepan, heat the canola oil over a medium heat. When it is hot, but not smoking, fry the onion and garlic for 5 minutes, until softened. Add the tomatoes, tomato paste, chillies, stock cube, sugar and coriander. Season with salt and pepper. Bring to the boil, cover, turn the heat down, and simmer for 20 minutes. If it thickens too much, add a little water. Keep warm while you prepare the filling.

To make the filling, in a large frying pan, heat 1 tablespoon oil and sauté the onion and pepper for 5–10 minutes over a medium heat, until softened. Remove from the pan and set aside.

Add a little more oil if necessary and add the sliced chicken. Sauté for 5–10 minutes until browned and almost cooked through. Transfer to a large bowl and add the onion and pepper, the whole kernel corn and half the salsa. Stir to combine. Add a little more oil to the frying pan and fry each tortilla before adding the filling. This prevents the tortilla soaking up too much liquid. Drain on paper towels and keep warm. To make the enchiladas, dip 1 tortilla in the sauce, remove and put on a warm plate. Add a little of the filling to the tortilla, sprinkle with a little cheese and roll up. Repeat with 2 more tortillas. Spoon a little sauce over the top, plus more cheese on top of that. Keep warm in the oven while you make the rest. Serve with soured cream and lime wedges on the side.

Serves 6

chicken & chorizo pasta with mediterranean vegetables

see variations page 186

Chicken and chorizo in a rich tomato sauce make a delicious and spicy pasta dish.

4 tbsp olive oil, divided
450 g (1 lb) diced aubergine
1 courgette, diced
1 red pepper, seeded and cut into
    2.5-cm (1-in) pieces
4 boneless, skinless chicken breasts,
    sliced diagonally
1/2 tsp paprika
110 g (4 oz) chorizo sausage

400 g (14 oz) GF penne pasta
tomato sauce, double quantity (page 148)
70 g (2 1/2 oz) quartered
    sun-dried tomatoes
3 tbsp freshly chopped basil, plus extra to serve
salt and freshly ground black pepper
few wafer-thin slices Parmesan cheese, to serve

Preheat the oven to 190°C (375°F/Gas mark 5). Place half the oil in a roasting tin and heat for 5 minutes. Add the aubergine, courgette and red pepper and turn them around in the oil. Roast for 25 minutes or until slightly chargrilled on the edges. Remove from the oven and set aside. In a large frying pan, heat the remaining oil, add the chicken and sprinkle with the paprika. Fry for about 10 minutes, until browned all over, add the chorizo and cook for 5 minutes more, until both the chicken and chorizo are cooked through. Set aside. In a large saucepan three-quarters full of boiling water, simmer the pasta for 10 minutes. Drain, rinse with cold water and set aside. Place the tomato sauce in the saucepan and heat until just simmering. Add the sun-dried tomatoes, aubergine, courgette, pepper, chicken and chorizo and basil. Season with salt and pepper and heat through. Serve sprinkled with basil and Parmesan.

Serves 4

pad thai

see variations page 187

This is one of Thailand's national dishes – stir-fried prawns and chicken, with tamarind, eggs and fish sauce, with coriander and chilli added for colour and heat.

450 g (1 lb) rice noodles
(ribbon if you can find
them)
juice of 2 limes
½ tsp cayenne pepper
1 tbsp brown sugar
2 tbsp fish sauce
2 tsp soya sauce
1 tsp cornflour
½ tsp tamarind paste

2 tbsp vegetable oil
2 boneless, skinless chicken
breasts, in 2.5-cm (1-in)
cubes
2 cloves garlic
1 small red onion, sliced
110 g (4 oz) bean sprouts
230 g (8 oz) cooked large
prawns

60 g (2 oz) finely chopped
salted peanuts
110 g (4 oz) chopped
coriander
freshly ground black pepper
2 medium red chillies,
finely chopped
2 limes, cut into wedges,
to serve

Put the noodles in a large bowl, cover with boiling water and leave for 4 minutes. Drain and refresh under cold water. Set aside.

In a medium bowl, mix the lime juice with the cayenne pepper, brown sugar, fish sauce, soya sauce, cornflour and tamarind paste. Stir to combine. In a large frying pan, heat the oil and fry the chicken for 5 minutes, until browned. Remove from the frying pan and set aside. Add the garlic and onion to the pan and cook over a medium heat for 5 minutes. Add the noodles and stir to heat through. Add the lime juice mixture, then stir in the bean sprouts, prawns, half the peanuts and coriander, black pepper and the chillies. Return the chicken to the pan and cook for 5 minutes, until everything is piping hot. Serve sprinkled with the remaining peanuts and coriander and garnished with lime wedges.

Serves 4

luxury fish pie

see variations page 188

Creamy mashed potato topping on poached fish in a parsley sauce is a real winner for the whole family and freezes really well.

for the potatoes
900 g (2 lbs) russet potatoes, peeled and cut into chunks
90 ml (3 fl. oz) full-fat milk
2 tbsp (1 oz) butter
salt and freshly ground black pepper

for the fish
230 g (8 oz) firm white skinless and boneless fish fillet, such as cod
230 g (8 oz) skinless and boneless salmon fillet

110 g (¼ lb) smoked skinless and boneless fish fillet
325 ml (11 fl. oz) full-fat milk
1 bay leaf
1 fish stock cube
1 tbsp (½ oz) butter, plus a little extra for greasing
1 shallot, finely chopped
1 tbsp white rice flour
3 tbsp freshly chopped parsley
110 g (¼ lb) cooked and peeled large prawns

Preheat the oven to 175°C (350°F/Gas mark 4) and grease a shallow ovenproof baking dish. Boil the potatoes in a large saucepan three-quarters filled with water for 20 minutes or until tender. Drain, return to the pan and place back over a very low heat for 3 minutes to dry out. Mash, add the milk and butter and beat until smooth. Season to taste with salt and pepper. Set aside. Check the fish for small bones and cut into large chunks. Place in a large frying pan; add the milk, bay leaf and stock cube; and simmer very gently for about 8 minutes or until just tender. With a slotted spoon, carefully lift the fish out of the frying pan onto a plate and drain the milk into a jug. In a medium saucepan, melt the butter and sauté the shallot for 5 minutes over a gentle heat, until softened.

Add the flour and stir together with the butter to make a roux. Cook for 2 minutes and gradually add the milk, stirring continuously until all the milk has been incorporated and the sauce has thickened. Taste, adjust the seasoning if necessary and add the parsley. Carefully add the fish and the prawns, folding them in gently and transfer to the shallow baking dish.

Spoon the mashed potatoes on top, covering all the fish and the sauce and roughing up the surface with a fork. Bake in the oven for 35 minutes, until the top is golden brown and the dish is piping hot. Serve immediately.

Serves 6

fish in crispy batter with oven-roasted chipped potatoes

see variations page 189

The batter is made using sparkling water, which makes it light and crispy.

for the potatoes
900 g (2 lbs) potatoes
2 tbsp olive oil
freshly ground black pepper

for the fish
1 tbsp white rice flour, for dredging
4 equal-size pieces of skinless and boneless
   firm white fish fillet, such as cod

50 g (1¾ oz) white rice flour
50 g (1¾ oz) cornflour
1 tsp baking powder
salt and freshly ground black pepper
1 egg white
120 ml (4 fl. oz) plus 2 tbsp ice-cold
   sparkling water
650 ml (22 fl. oz) sunflower oil, for frying
cooked peas and lemon wedges, to serve

Preheat the oven to 200°C (400°F/Gas mark 6). Peel the potatoes, cut into 2-cm (¾-in)-thick slices, then cut each slice into 2-cm (¾-in) strips, making thick chips. Place in a large bowl, dry slightly with paper towels and season with plenty of coarsely ground black pepper. Add half the olive oil and stir with a wooden spoon to evenly coat the chips with oil. Grease a baking tray with the remaining olive oil and place it in the oven for 5 minutes to heat. Then, evenly spread the potatoes on the tray and roast for about 35 minutes, until golden and cooked through.

While the potatoes are baking, prepare the fish. Place the tablespoon of rice flour onto a plate. Dry the fish with paper towels and dredge in the rice flour.

In a large bowl, mix the rest of the rice flour, the cornflour, baking powder, salt and pepper. Pour the oil for frying into a wok or large pan and heat to 200°C (400°F/Gas mark 6), checking the heat with a thermometer. In a medium bowl, whisk the egg white until frothy, but not too stiff. Make a well in the centre of the flour mixture and pour in the sparkling water, whisking lightly. Add the egg white and whisk again briefly, keeping the bubbles so the batter stays light. Dip a piece of fish in the batter to coat and carefully transfer with a slotted spoon into the hot oil. Fry each piece of fish for 5–6 minutes and lift out with a slotted spoon to drain on paper towels. Keep warm while you fry the remaining fish. Serve with the chipped potatoes, with cooked peas on the side and garnished with a wedge of fresh lemon.

Serves 4

potato pissaladière

see variations page 190

Originating in France, this dish uses mashed potatoes instead of pizza dough as a base. It makes a great vegetarian main dish.

2 tbsp (1 oz) butter, plus extra for greasing
570 g (1¼ lbs) potatoes, peeled and cut into
    chunks
1 large egg, lightly beaten
2 tbsp finely shredded Parmesan cheese
salt and freshly ground black pepper
2 tbsp sun-dried tomato paste

2 tbsp tomato paste
3 tomatoes, thinly sliced
2 tbsp freshly chopped basil
60 g (2 oz) shredded mozzarella cheese
60 g (2 oz) shredded Cheddar cheese
1 60-g (2-oz) tin anchovy fillets, drained on a
    paper towel

Grease a baking tray with a little butter and preheat the oven to 200°C (400°F/Gas mark 6). Boil the potatoes in a large saucepan three-quarters filled with water for 20 minutes, until tender. Drain, return to the pan and place over a gentle heat for 5 minutes to dry out. Mash, then add the butter, egg, Parmesan cheese, salt and pepper. Beat until smooth. Spread the mashed potatoes over the greased baking tray to a rectangle about 20x30 cm (8x11 in). Bake for 20 minutes and remove from the oven.

In a medium bowl, mix the sun-dried tomato paste and tomato paste and spread over the potato base. Arrange the tomato slices, basil, mozzarella and Cheddar cheese on top. Slice each anchovy fillet in half and arrange in a lattice pattern on top of the cheese. Add the olives and bake for about 10 minutes or until the cheese has melted. Serve immediately, cut into squares.

Serves 4

mixed vegetable lasagna

see variations page 191

Without fail, everyone loves lasagna and this version, with grilled vegetables, puttanesca sauce and pesto-infused ricotta cheese, is packed with flavour.

450 g (1 lb) GF lasagna noodles

450 g (1 lb) ricotta cheese

for the puttanesca sauce
tomato sauce, double quantity (page 148)
170 g (6 oz) pitted black olives
1 tbsp capers, drained
1 tbsp finely chopped anchovies, drained
$1/_2$ tsp dried red chilli flakes

for the pesto oil
2 cloves garlic, crushed
large handful freshly torn basil leaves
120 ml (4 fl. oz) extra-virgin olive oil
1 tbsp finely shredded Parmesan cheese
salt and freshly ground black pepper

for the filling
1 large onion, roughly chopped
1 medium courgette, cut into 0.5-cm ($1/_4$-in) slices
1 red pepper, seeded and cut into 2.5-cm (1-in) pieces
1 yellow pepper, seeded and cut into 2.5-cm (1-in) pieces
1 aubergine (about 13 cm (5 in) long), cut into 2.5-cm (1-in) cubes
3 tbsp olive oil
230 g (8 oz) mozzarella cheese, shredded

Cook the lasagna noodles as directed on the packet. Drain, refresh in cold water and leave to dry on clean kitchen towels. In a large bowl, mix all puttanesca sauce ingredients and set aside.

To make the pesto oil, in a food processor, process the garlic, basil, olive oil, Parmesan cheese and salt and pepper until the basil leaves are finely chopped and incorporated into the oil. In a large bowl, mix the ricotta cheese with most of the pesto oil. Set the rest aside.

Preheat the grill. Put the onion, courgette, peppers and aubergine into a large bowl, drizzle with the olive oil and stir to coat all over. Season with salt and pepper and spread out on a baking tray. Grill for about 5 minutes per side or until slightly chargrilled on the edges and cooked through. Allow to cool slightly.

Preheat the oven to 175°C (350°F/Gas mark 4). In a large, shallow greased ovenproof baking dish, spread sauce across the bottom of the dish. Add a layer of lasagne, a layer of ricotta and pesto oil, a layer of mixed vegetables, a layer of mozzarella and a layer of sauce. Repeat until all the ingredients have been used up, finishing with the mozzarella. Bake for 1 hour 15 minutes, until golden and bubbling. Leave to rest for 10 minutes. Serve drizzled with pesto oil.

Serves 6

polenta pizza with bacon, mushrooms & spinach

see variations page 192

Polenta is amazingly versatile. Here it is used as a pizza base, topped with mushrooms and spinach and enhanced with lots of herbs and spices.

2 tbsp canola oil, plus extra for greasing
120 ml (4 fl. oz) whole milk
600 ml (20 fl. oz) chicken stock
1 tsp salt
freshly ground black pepper
110 g (4 oz) coarse cornmeal (polenta)

230 g (8 oz) sliced mushrooms
60 g (2 oz) fresh spinach leaves
110 g (4 oz) Cheddar cheese, finely shredded
1 tomato, sliced and each slice quartered
6 strips bacon, cooked until crispy and chopped

Generously grease a baking tray with oil. In a large saucepan, over a medium heat, combine milk, stock and salt. Bring almost to the boil and gradually pour in the cornmeal, whisking continuously. Reduce heat and simmer gently, stirring continuously until the mixture is the consistency of thick oatmeal. Add a little water if needed. Stir in 1 tablespon oil, then spread the polenta on the baking tray to a thickness of about 1.3 cm (½ in), to form a circle. Cover with clingfilm and chill for at least an hour or overnight. Heat the oven to 230°C (450°F/Gas mark 8). Remove clingfilm and bake the base in the oven for about 25 minutes, until nicely browned. Meanwhile, in a large frying pan, heat 1 tablespoon oil, add the mushrooms and cook gently for about 10 minutes. Add the spinach to wilt. Drain for 3 minutes on a plate covered with kitchen towel and sprinkle with salt and pepper. Remove base from the oven and spread with cheese, mushrooms and spinach. Add tomatoes and bacon and bake for 5 minutes. Serve immediately.

Serves 4

pan-fried cod with garlic & cannellini mash

see variations page 193

Crispy on the outside, white and flaky on the inside, this fish is served with garlic-infused mashed cannellini beans.

4 thick skinless and boneless white fish fillets,
    such as cod
2 tbsp white rice flour
2 tbsp cornflour
salt and freshly ground black pepper
6 tbsp olive oil
1 small onion, finely chopped

2 cloves garlic, crushed
2 450-g (16-oz) tins cannellini beans, drained
3 tbsp freshly chopped parsley, plus extra
    to serve
3 tbsp water
lemon wedges, to serve

Check the fish for bones. On a large plate, mix the rice flour and cornflour and add the salt and pepper. Dredge the fish fillets in the flour and set aside. In a medium saucepan, heat 1 tablespoon olive oil, add the onion and garlic and cook over a gentle heat for 5 minutes or until softened. Add the cannellini beans and cook for 5 minutes, until heated through. Transfer to a food processor, add the parsley and 3 tablespoons olive oil and blend until smooth. Return to the pan, add the water and season to taste with salt and pepper. Cover and keep warm. In a large frying pan, heat the remaining olive oil and when it is hot, but not smoking, add the fish fillets and fry over a high heat for 2–3 minutes per side, until a golden crust forms. Serve immediately, placed on top of the cannellini mash, garnished with extra parsley and with a lemon wedge on the side to squeeze over the fish.

Serves 4

sweet & sour pork balls

see variations page 194

The batter for these pork balls is wonderfully light and tasty. They are accompanied by a delicious sweet and sour sauce. Steamed rice is good with this recipe.

for the sauce
110 g (4 oz) tomato ketchup
2 tsp soya sauce
120 ml (4 fl. oz) white vinegar
180 ml (6 fl. oz) water
300 g (10 oz) caster sugar
85 g (3 oz) brown sugar
3 tbsp cornflour
60 ml (2 fl. oz) water

for the pork balls
90 g (3¹/₃ oz) white rice flour
60 g (2 oz) potato starch
2 tbsp tapioca flour
110 g (4 oz) cornflour
1 tsp baking powder
1 tsp bicarbonate of soda
1 tsp sugar
about 240 ml (8 fl. oz) water
canola oil for frying
900 g (2 lbs) lean pork cut into 2.5-cm
    (1-in) cubes

First make the sauce. In a medium saucepan, combine ketchup, soya sauce, vinegar, water and both sugars. Stirring continuously, simmer for 5 minutes. In a small bowl, mix together the cornflour and water and add to the sauce. Stirring continuously, simmer until thickened. Keep warm while you make the pork balls. In a large bowl, mix together the rice flour, potato starch, tapioca flour, cornflour, baking powder, bicarbonate of soda and sugar. Make a well in the centre and add enough water to make a fairly thick batter. Dry the pork with kitchen towel. Fill a large saucepan with about 7–10 cm (3–4 in) oil. Heat until it is 190°C (375°F/Gas mark 5). Dip each piece of pork into the batter and drop it carefully into the oil. Fry in small batches for 5 minutes until golden brown. Remove with a slotted spoon to drain on paper towels. Serve with the sauce.

Serves 6

spicy moroccan chicken tagine

see variations page 195

On a cold winter's evening, there is something very warming about a tagine and the addition of ginger and cinnamon adds an exotic touch, evocative of warm Moroccan nights.

8 skinless and boneless chicken thighs
2 tbsp cornflour
salt and freshly ground black pepper
2 tbsp canola oil or olive oil
2 medium red onions, finely chopped
2 cloves garlic, crushed
1 tsp ground ginger
1 tsp ground cumin

½ tsp ground cinnamon
3 lemons
300 ml (10 fl. oz) good-quality
   chicken stock
1 tbsp honey
1 chicken stock cube
8 green olives, pitted
2 tbsp freshly chopped coriander

Preheat the oven to 175°C (350°F/Gas mark 4). Trim the chicken thighs of any residual fat and bone. Put the cornflour onto a plate, season with salt and pepper and add the chicken, turning it around to coat all over. In a large frying pan, heat the oil and cook the onions and garlic for 5 minutes, until softened. Add the ground ginger, cumin and cinnamon. Stir to combine and cook for 3 minutes. Cut the lemons into quarters, add to the frying pan and cook for 3 minutes more. Add any remaining cornflour, stir and add the stock and honey, stirring continuously. Sprinkle in the stock cube, stir and transfer to a large casserole dish.

Cover and bake in the oven for about 1 hour, until all the flavours are blended together and the chicken is cooked through. Remove from the oven and stir in the olives and coriander. Taste to check the seasoning, adjusting if necessary. Serve immediately.

Serves 4

beef in red wine sauce with mushrooms

see base recipe page 141

beef in red wine sauce with red kidney beans & chilli

Prepare the basic recipe, omitting 110 g (4 oz) beef and substituting
1 400-g (14-oz) tin red kidney beans in chilli sauce and adding 2 teaspoons
medium chilli powder.

beef in red wine sauce with horseradish dumplings

Prepare the basic recipe. Make horseradish dumplings by mixing 40 g
(1½ oz) white rice flour, 60 g (2 oz) cornflour, 110 g (4 oz) frozen and
shredded butter, 2 tablespoons horseradish cream, salt, freshly ground black
pepper and enough water to make a soft dough. Roll into 8 balls and drop
into the top of the casserole 15 minutes before the end of cooking time.

beef in port wine sauce with peppers & aubergine

Prepare the basic recipe, replacing 120 ml (4 fl. oz) red wine with port
wine. Omit 110 g (4 oz) mushrooms and add ½ red and ½ green peppers,
seeded and sliced and 110 g (4 oz) cubed aubergine to the frying pan with
the mushrooms.

beef in red wine sauce with juniper berries

Prepare the basic recipe, adding 1 tablespoon juniper berries to the frying
pan with the onion.

savoury beef tarts with crispy potato topping

see base recipe page 142

chicken & mushroom tart with potato topping
Prepare the basic recipe, replacing the beef, beef stock and beef stock cube with
450 g (1 lb) cubed boneless chicken breasts, chicken stock and chicken stock
cube. Add 110 g (4 oz) chopped mushrooms with the onion.

lamb & rosemary tart with potato topping
Prepare the basic recipe, replacing the beef, beef stock and beef stock cube with
450 g (1 lb) ground lamb, chicken stock and lamb or chicken stock cube. Replace
the Italian herbs with rosemary.

sausage, tomato, & bean tart with potato topping
Prepare the basic recipe, replacing the beef, beef stock and beef stock cube with
340 g (12 oz) finely chopped Italian sausage, 120 ml (4 fl. oz) chicken stock
and chicken stock cube. Add 1 450-g (16-oz) tin beans in tomato sauce with
the stock.

cheese & onion tart with crispy topping
Prepare the basic recipe, omitting all meat ingredients. Add 2 tablespoons butter,
1 finely chopped and sautéed onion, 140 g (5 oz) shredded Cheddar cheese to
900 g (2 lb) mashed potatoes. Season well. Spoon into crusts, sprinkle with
cheese and bake for 20 minutes. Grill for 2–3 minutes to crisp.

variations

breaded fried chicken with parmesan

see base recipe page 145

breaded fried chicken with citrus rum sauce

Prepare the basic recipe, serving it with a hot citrus sauce. In a little oil, sauté 2 tablespoons each diced onion, carrot and celery until softened. Add 1 tablespoon tomato paste, 1 crushed clove garlic, 1 bay leaf, 1 teaspoon black pepper, 240 ml (8 fl. oz) beef stock, 355 ml (12 fl. oz) orange juice, 60 ml (2 fl. oz) each of dark rum and thick cream. Simmer, covered, for 30 minutes, then thicken with a little diluted cornflour. Season to taste.

breaded coconut prawns

Prepare the basic recipe, replacing the chicken with 450 g (1 lb) medium prawns and the breadcrumbs with 170 g (6 oz) shredded coconut.

breaded fried chicken with pizza sauce & mozzarella

Prepare the basic recipe, adding 2 tablespoons pizza sauce (page 112) and 2 slices mozzarella to each breast 10 minutes before the end of baking time.

dairy-free breaded fried chicken with oats & almonds

Prepare the basic recipe, replacing the Parmesan with 30 g (1 oz) chopped almonds and the breadcrumbs with 170 g (6 oz) rolled oats.

variations

steak & onion pie

see base recipe page 146

steak & onion pie with roast chestnuts
Prepare the basic recipe, adding 450 g (1 lb) roasted chestnuts. To roast them, make a shallow incision in the skin on each side. Roast on a baking tray at 190°C (375°F/Gas mark 5) for 25 minutes. Cool slightly. Peel off skins, then add to the beef and onion mixture.

chicken pot pie with spring vegetables
Prepare the basic recipe, using a white sauce (page 89) and adding 340 g (12 oz) diced cooked chicken and 450 g (1 lb) cooked spring vegetables in the pie.

cheese & onion pie with chives
Instead of the base recipe, layer sliced and cooked potatoes with slices of Cheddar cheese and thinly sliced onions. Add salt, pepper and snipped fresh chives to each layer. Top with pastry as in the base recipe.

steak & baby onion pie with juniper berries
Prepare the basic recipe, replacing the large onions with 340 g (12 oz) baby onions. Add 1 tablespoon juniper berries before baking.

variations

beef cannelloni with tomato sauce

see base recipe page 148

spinach & ricotta cannelloni with tomato sauce
Prepare the basic recipe, omitting the beef filling. Substitute
450 g (1 lb) ricotta cheese, mixed with 110 g (4 oz) cooked,
cooled and chopped spinach and seasoned to taste with salt and
freshly ground black pepper.

chicken & spinach cannelloni with tomato sauce
Prepare the basic recipe, replacing the beef with ground chicken
and adding 60 g (2 oz) cooked, cooled and chopped spinach to
the frying pan with the cheese.

cannelloni with spinach, walnuts & mascarpone
Prepare the basic recipe, replacing half the beef with 230 g (8 oz)
mascarpone cheese and adding 40 g (1½ oz) chopped walnuts to
the frying pan with the cheese.

dairy-free beef cannelloni with tomato sauce
Prepare the basic recipe, replacing the cheese in both the beef
filling and the tomato sauce with dairy-free cheese. Grease the
dish and foil with oil, not butter. Omit the Parmesan to serve.

variations

roast rack of lamb with gremolata & asparagus

see base recipe page 150

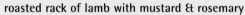

roasted rack of lamb with mustard & rosemary

Prepare the basic recipe, omitting the gremolata. Season the lamb, spread with 2 tablespoons Dijon mustard and sprinkle with 1 tablespoon dried rosemary. Brown and roast as before.

roasted rack of lamb with moroccan spices

Prepare the basic recipe, omitting the gremolata, salt and black pepper. Season the lamb with Moroccan spice blend as follows. Mix together 1 teaspoon each of ground cumin, ground ginger, salt and black pepper, $\frac{1}{2}$ teaspoon each of ground cinnamon, ground coriander, cayenne pepper, ground allspice and ground cloves. Brown and roast as before.

roasted rack of lamb with kashmiri spices

Prepare the basic recipe, omitting the gremolata. Season the lamb with salt, black pepper and 1 tablespoon Garam Masala. Brown and roast as before.

variations

slow-roasted lamb shoulder

see base recipe page 152

slow-roasted pork belly

Prepare the basic recipe, omitting the lamb and rosemary. Substitute a pork
belly and 3 sprigs each of fresh thyme and sage. Place the pork skin-side up
on the vegetables. Use a chicken stock cube. After cooking 3 hours, remove
foil, turn the heat back up to 200°C (400°F/Gas mark 6) and cook for 20
minutes or until the skin is crispy.

slow-roasted chicken & onion bake

Prepare the basic recipe, omitting the lamb and rosemary. Use a large
chicken, jointed into 6 portions and 3 sprigs each of thyme and sage.
Cook for 2 hours only. Remove foil for last 20 minutes to brown the skin.

slow-roasted beef brisket

Prepare the basic recipe, replacing the lamb with beef brisket. Use beef
stock and beef stock cube. Add 1 400-g (14-oz) tin drained butter beans to
the vegetables.

slow-roasted pomegranate treacle lamb shoulder

Prepare the basic recipe, omitting the rosemary and garlic. Drizzle
90 ml (3 fl. oz) pomegranate treacle dressing (page 218) over
the lamb before roasting.

jerk chicken with mango salsa

see base recipe page 155

lemon & garlic chicken
Prepare the basic recipe, omitting the jerk seasoning and mango salsa. Sauté 2 finely chopped cloves garlic in the oil before adding the chicken. Squeeze the juice of 1 lemon over the chicken just before the end of cooking time.

jerk chicken with aïoli
Prepare the basic recipe, replacing the mango salsa with aïoli. In a small bowl, mix 230 g (8 oz) good-quality mayonnaise with 2 minced cloves garlic.

jerk chicken with pineapple salsa
Prepare the basic recipe, replacing the mango salsa with pineapple salsa. In a medium bowl, mix together 3 tablespoons brown sugar, 2 tablespoons soya sauce, 230 g (8 oz) finely chopped fresh pineapple, 3 tablespoons freshly chopped coriander and 1 finely chopped red chilli. Keep covered and chilled until ready to serve.

chicken with cajun seasoning
Prepare the basic recipe, substituting Cajun seasoning for the jerk seasoning.

variations

chicken korma

see base recipe page 156

medium chicken balti
Prepare the basic recipe, omitting the almonds and coconut milk. Substitute
1 400-g (14-oz) tin chopped tomatoes in juice and add 1 teaspoon each of
ground cinnamon, garam masala and chilli powder. Add 60 g (2 oz) freshly
chopped coriander just before serving.

mild goan chicken curry
Omit the almonds. Add 1 teaspoon each of ground mustard seeds and
paprika. Add 1 tablespoon lemon juice just before serving.

chicken curry with spinach
Prepare the basic recipe, omitting the almonds and coconut milk. Add to the
sauce 3 quartered tomatoes, the seeds of 3 cardamom pods, 2 teaspoons
garam masala and 60 g (2 oz) fresh spinach. Just before serving, stir in 30 g
(1 oz) freshly chopped coriander and 4 tablespoons plain yogurt.

dairy-free medium chicken dhansak
Prepare the basic recipe, omitting the ground almonds and coconut milk.
Add 1 400-g (14-oz) tin green lentils, drained; 1 400-g (14-oz) tin chopped
tomatoes in juice; and 2 teaspoons medium chilli powder. Replace the butter
in the rice with canola oil.

variations

chicken enchiladas

see base recipe page 158

enchiladas with creamy chicken filling
Prepare the basic recipe, omitting the chicken filling. Mix 8 chopped spring
onions, 340 g (12 oz) finely sliced and sautéed mushrooms, 450 g (1 lb) diced
cooked chicken, 110 g (4 oz) whole kernel corn, pinch chilli powder and 230 g
(8 oz) soured cream. Fill enchiladas as before.

enchiladas with beef
Prepare the basic recipe, replacing the chicken with 500 g (18 oz) ground
beef.

scrambled egg enchiladas
Prepare the basic recipe, the chicken filling. Substitute 8 eggs, scrambled and
cooked with 6 finely chopped spring onions, 2 finely chopped green chillies,
60 g (2 oz) freshly chopped coriander and 4 finely chopped tomatoes. Season
with salt and pepper.

enchiladas with mixed bean salad
Prepare the basic recipe. In a large bowl, mix 1 400-g (14-oz) tin each of
red kidney beans, pinto beans, green beans and whole kernel corn, all drained.
Add 60 g (2 oz) freshly chopped coriander, 2 tablespoons lime juice, 2
teaspoons honey, 90 ml (3 fl. oz) olive oil and 110 g (4 oz) shredded lettuce.

variations

chicken & chorizo pasta with mediterranean vegetables

see base recipe page 161

sausage, spinach & olive pasta with basil
Prepare the basic recipe, omitting 1 chicken breast and the chorizo. Brown 230 g (8 oz) Italian sausage, crumbled, with the chicken. Add 60 g (2 oz) fresh spinach and 8 pitted black olives 5 minutes before serving.

crab & prawns pasta with creamy tomato sauce
Prepare the basic recipe, replacing the chicken and chorizo with 230 g (8 oz) crabmeat and 230 g (8 oz) medium prawns. Just before serving, stir in 3 tablespoons thick cream.

goat's cheese, spinach & pine nut pasta
Prepare the basic recipe, omitting the chicken, chorizo and aubergine. Add 230 g (8 oz) cubed goat's cheese, 60 g (2 oz) fresh spinach and 40 g (1½ oz) pine nuts to the saucepan just before serving.

mushroom & garlic pasta with cherry tomatoes
Prepare the basic recipe, omitting 2 chicken breasts and the chorizo. Add 450 g (1 lb) chopped mushrooms to the frying pan when the chicken has browned. Cook for 5 minutes. Add 8 cherry tomatoes to heat with the tomato sauce.

pad thai

see base recipe page 162

pad thai with coconut rice
Prepare the basic recipe and serve with coconut rice. In a large saucepan
three-quarters full of boiling water, cook 255 g (9 oz) jasmine rice for
10 minutes. Drain and return to the pan. Stir in 2 tablespoons coconut
cream paste over a gentle heat until melted into the rice. Serve immediately.

stir-fried chicken & prawns in black bean sauce
Prepare the basic recipe, omitting the lime juice, brown sugar, fish sauce and
peanuts. Add 3 tablespoons black beans, 2 tablespoons soya sauce, 1
teaspoon sugar and 2 tablespoons chicken stock with the prawns.

thai green chicken curry
Prepare the basic recipe, omitting the noodles, lime juice, cayenne pepper,
brown sugar and tamarind paste. Substitute 2 tablespoons green Thai curry
paste, 1 400-g (14-oz) tin coconut milk and 170 g (6 oz) cooked and
chopped fine green beans. Omit the prawns, beansprouts and peanuts and
add 2 extra chicken breasts. Serve with coconut rice (see above).

pad thai with bok choy
Prepare the basic recipe. Cut the base off the bok choy, wash and chop it
finely. Add to the frying pan with the garlic and onion.

variations

luxury fish pie

see base recipe page 164

luxury fish pie with swordfish & sweet potato mash
Prepare the basic recipe, replacing the smoked fish with skinless and boneless swordfish. Replace half the potatoes with sweet potatoes.

luxury fish & corn pie topped with creamy cheese mash
Prepare the basic recipe, replacing the milk with single cream. Add 85 g (3 oz) drained whole kernel corn to the sauce and sprinkle 3 tablespoons Cheddar cheese over the potatoes before baking.

luxury fish pie with leeks
Prepare the basic recipe, adding 1 finely chopped leek to the pan with the shallot.

luxury fish pie with eggs
Prepare the basic recipe, folding 3 chopped hard-boiled eggs into the sauce with the fish.

dairy-free luxury fish pie topped with creamy mashed potatoes
Prepare the basic recipe, replacing the milk and butter in the potatoes and sauce with rice or almond milk and dairy-free margarine.

variations

fish in crispy batter with oven-roasted chipped potatoes

see base recipe page 166

fish in crispy batter with crushed peas
Prepare the basic recipe. Boil 500 g (18 oz) fresh or frozen peas until tender. Drain and return to pan. Add 1 tablespoon freshly chopped parsley, 1 tablespoon freshly chopped mint and 2 teaspoons thick cream. Roughly mix with a hand blender or mash lightly with a potato masher.

fish in crispy batter with petit pois à la français
Prepare the basic recipe. In a large saucepan, sauté 3 chopped strips of bacon with 4 chopped spring onions. Add 1 shredded head Little Gem (baby Romaine) lettuce and cook 4 minutes. Add 120 ml (4 fl. oz) chicken stock and 500 g (18 oz) fresh or frozen petit pois or peas, then simmer gently for about 7 minutes, until tender and stock has reduced. Serve with the fish.

fish in crispy batter with tartar sauce
Prepare the basic recipe. In a medium bowl, mix 230 g (8 oz) good-quality mayonnaise with 2 tablespoons rinsed capers, 2 tablespoons chopped mini gherkins, 2 tablespoons freshly chopped parsley, 1 teaspoon lemon juice and salt and freshly ground black pepper to taste.

potato pissaladière

see base recipe page 168

sweet potato pissaladière
Prepare the basic recipe, substituting sweet potatoes for half the potatoes in the base.

potato & rutabaga pissaladière with pepperoni
Prepare the basic recipe, substituting rutabaga for half the potatoes in the base. Omit the anchovies and olives and add a few slices of pepperoni under the cheese.

potato & squash pissaladière with mushrooms
Prepare the basic recipe, using chopped butternut squash in place of half the potatoes in the base. Omit the anchovies and olives and add a layer of lightly sautéed sliced mushrooms under the cheese.

dairy-free potato pissaladière
Prepare the basic recipe, replacing the butter and cheeses with dairy-free margarine and dairy-free cheese.

variations

mixed vegetable lasagna

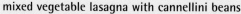
see base recipe page 170

mixed vegetable lasagna with cannellini beans
Prepare the basic recipe, adding 170 g (6 oz) drained cannellini beans to the
cooked mixed vegetables before layering in the dish.

mixed vegetable & seafood lasagna
Prepare the basic recipe, adding an extra layer of 170 g (6 oz) cooked mixed
seafood, such as prawns, mahi mahi and crab to the dish.

lasagna with ground beef
Prepare the basic recipe, replacing the mixed vegetables with the ground
beef filling from the beef cannelloni (page 148).

mixed vegetable lasagna with chicken & corn
Prepare the basic recipe, adding an extra layer of 170 g (6 oz) seasoned,
cooked and diced chicken and 170 g (6 oz) whole kernel corn to the dish.

mixed spring vegetable lasagna
Prepare the basic recipe, omitting the grilled vegetables. Substitute a
selection of lightly steamed spring vegetables, such as broccoli, asparagus,
celery, peas and sugar snap peas.

polenta pizza with bacon, mushrooms & spinach

see base recipe page 172

polenta pizza with caramelised onion & goat's cheese

Prepare the basic recipe, omitting the cheese and bacon. Substitute 230 g (8 oz) caramelised onions (page 101) and 60 g (2 oz) cubed goat's cheese.

meat lovers polenta pizza with extra pepperoni & chilli

Prepare the basic recipe, adding about 9 slices of pepperoni and sprinkling with 1 finely chopped red chilli.

polenta pizza with sausage & pepper

Prepare the basic recipe, omitting the bacon. Substitute 85 g (3 oz) cooked and crumbled sausage and ½ a thinly sliced and lightly sautéed red pepper.

dairy-free polenta pizza

Prepare the basic recipe, replacing the whole milk with oat or rice milk. Omit the cheese.

pan-fried cod with garlic & cannellini mash

see base recipe page 173

pan-fried mahi mahi with mango salsa
Prepare the basic recipe, using mahi mahi and serve with mango salsa (page 155).

pan-fried tilapia with crumb topping
Prepare the basic recipe, using tilapia. Make a crumb topping by mixing 60 g (2 oz) GF breadcrumbs, 40 g (1½ oz) Parmesan cheese, 2 tablespoons freshly chopped parsley, 1 tablespoon lime juice, salt, and pepper. Spread over the tilapia and fry gently in a little oil, for 5–6 minutes, until fish is just cooked.

pan-fried coconut prawns with sweet chilli sauce
Instead of the basic recipe, roll 450 g (1 lb) peeled and cooked large prawns in white rice flour, dip in beaten egg and roll in shredded coconut. Pan-fry in canola oil for 4–5 minutes per side. Serve with chilli sauce.

pan-fried mild mustard fish burgers
Instead of the basic recipe, roughly chop the fish and mix with 2 tablespoons Dijon mustard. Season and form into 4 burgers. Dust with the flour, shaking off excess. Cook 2–3 minutes per side in a little olive oil.

variations

sweet & sour pork balls

see base recipe page 174

sweet & sour chicken balls
Prepare the basic recipe, replacing the pork with chicken breast cut into
2.5-cm (1-in) pieces.

sweet chilli chicken balls
Prepare the basic recipe, replacing the pork with chicken breast cut into
2.5-cm (1-in) pieces. For the sauce, replace 60 g (2 oz) ketchup with 60 g (2
oz) sweet chilli sauce.

sticky orange chicken balls
Prepare the basic recipe, replacing the pork with chicken breast cut into
2.5-cm (1-in) pieces. For the sauce, add the zest and juice of 1 orange and
replace the white sugar with brown sugar, making 310 g (11 oz) in total.

sweet & sour prawns balls
Prepare the basic recipe, replacing the pork with medium-sized prawns.

spicy moroccan chicken tagine

see base recipe page 175

spicy moroccan lamb & prune tagine
Prepare the basic recipe, omitting the chicken and 60 ml (2 fl. oz) chicken stock. Substitute 110 g (4 oz) diced lean lamb and 1 500 g (16-oz) tin pitted prunes, with the juice, added with the stock. If you cannot find prunes, use tinned apricots.

spicy pork tagine with green peppers
Prepare the basic recipe, replacing the chicken with 110 g (4 oz) diced pork. Add 1 seeded and sliced green pepper to the frying pan with the onion and garlic.

fruity moroccan chicken tagine with tomatoes & almonds
Prepare the basic recipe, replacing 240 ml (8 fl. oz) chicken stock with 1 500 g (16-oz) tin chopped tomatoes in juice. Add 1 tablespoon each of chopped dates, dried apricots, golden raisins and sliced almonds to the casserole dish before baking.

sides

Here you will find a variety of side dishes to complement and enhance the other recipes in this book. From potato casseroles to stuffed peppers and vegetable curry, there are plenty of ideas for inspiration.

stuffed peppers

see variations page 222

These peppers, with the fresh taste of herbs, make a lovely side dish. With more vitamin C than an orange, they are a great choice for children. Use at least two different colours of peppers to make an especially colourful dish.

120 ml (4 fl. oz) extra-virgin olive oil
1 large onion, finely chopped
2 cloves garlic, crushed
3 large tomatoes
170 g (6 oz) raw Arborio rice

4 tbsp freshly chopped parsley
2 tbsp freshly chopped dill
1 tbsp freshly chopped mint
coarse sea salt and freshly ground black pepper
6 large peppers, assorted red and yellow

Preheat the oven to 190°C (375°F/Gas mark 5).

In a large frying pan, heat 1 tablespoon of the olive oil and fry the onion and garlic for 5 minutes, until softened. Chop the tomatoes on a plate to retain the juice, add to the frying pan and stir to combine. Add the rice and herbs and season with salt and pepper.

Cut the stem end off each pepper and remove the seeds and ribs with your fingers. Tightly pack the peppers with the rice mixture, pressing down with your fingers. Replace the stem ends and lay the peppers on their sides in a roasting tin. Drizzle the rest of the olive oil over the peppers, sprinkle with coarse sea salt and add enough hot water to come halfway up the sides of the peppers. Bake, uncovered, in the oven for 70–90 minutes or until the rice is cooked and the peppers are slightly blackened on the edges. Serve immediately.

Serves 6

spicy potato wedges with soured cream dip

see variations page 223

Golden brown and with a slight spicy touch, these make a great side dish for chicken or beef or as an accompaniment to soup for a light lunch.

1 kg (2¼ lbs) potatoes
2 tbsp (1 oz) butter
1 tbsp Cajun seasoning
5 tbsp soured cream, for dipping

Grease a large baking tray with a little butter. Preheat the oven to 190°C (375°F/Gas mark 5).

Peel the potatoes and cut each one into 8 wedges. Three-quarters fill a large saucepan with water, add the potatoes and bring to the boil. Simmer for 5 minutes, drain and transfer to a large bowl. Add the butter and seasoning and stir lightly with a wooden spoon until the potatoes are well coated with both. Tip onto the baking tray and bake in the oven for about 25–30 minutes, until crisp and golden. Remove from the oven and serve immediately, with the soured cream for dipping.

Serves 6

green bean casserole with garlic & walnuts

see variations page 224

You will find that homemade mushroom sauce for green bean casserole is not only tastier than condensed mushroom soup, but so much healthier.

1 tsp vegetable oil, for greasing
560 g (1¼ lbs) fine green beans
60 g (2 oz) butter
1 small onion, finely chopped
2 cloves garlic, crushed
170 g (6 oz) finely sliced mushrooms
35 g (1¼ oz) white rice flour
415 ml (14 fl. oz) full-fat milk
1 tbsp soya sauce

1 chicken stock cube
salt and freshly ground black pepper
for the topping
1 tbsp canola oil
1 large onion, finely sliced
1 tbsp brown sugar
40 g (1½ oz) chopped walnuts
freshly grated Parmesan cheese, to serve

Grease a casserole dish with a little vegetable oil. In a large saucepan, blanch the green beans for 5 minutes, drain and refresh with cold water. Set aside. Melt the butter in the saucepan, add the onion and garlic and cook over a gentle heat for 10 minutes until softened. Add the mushrooms and cook for 5 minutes. Stir in the flour and cook for 3 minutes, stirring continuously. Gradually stir in the milk, incorporating it into the roux and vegetables slowly and cook over a gentle heat until the sauce has thickened. Add the soya sauce and chicken stock cube, stirring continuously. Taste the sauce and season with a little salt and plenty of black pepper. Preheat oven to 175°C (350°F/Gas mark 4). Put the drained beans into the casserole dish and pour the mushroom sauce over them. Cook for 20–25 minutes, stirring every 5 minutes.

Meanwhile, heat the canola oil in a large frying pan. When it is hot, but not smoking, add the sliced onion and cook over a gentle heat for 15 minutes. Add the brown sugar and continue to cook for about 10 minutes. Turn the heat up to high and cook for 2 minutes, stirring continuously, until the onions have browned and are caramelised. Remove from the heat and keep warm. When the beans are heated through, remove the casserole from the oven, top with the onions, sprinkle with the chopped walnuts and a little Parmesan cheese and serve immediately.

Serves 6

aubergine, tomato & courgette casserole

see variations page 225

Packed with flavour and reminiscent of warm summer evenings, this casserole is warming and comforting in all weather.

5 tbsp extra-virgin olive oil, plus extra
   for greasing
4 courgettes (18 cm (7 in) long), cut into
   1.3-cm ($\frac{1}{2}$-in) slices
6 ripe plum tomatoes, sliced
2 aubergines (18 cm (7 in) long), cut into
   0.6-cm ($\frac{1}{4}$-in) slices

4 cloves garlic, finely chopped
3 tbsp fresh rosemary leaves
salt and freshly ground black pepper
30 g (1 oz) finely shredded
   Parmesan cheese

Grease a round casserole dish with oil. Preheat the oven to 220°C (425°F/Gas mark 7).

In the casserole dish, make a layer of overlapping vegetable slices, using some of each vegetable in the layer. Sprinkle each layer with a little of the garlic, oil, rosemary, salt and pepper. Continue making layers until all the ingredients are used up. Drizzle the top with more olive oil, sprinkle with the Parmesan cheese and bake in the oven for 50–60 minutes.

Serves 4

crispy onion rings

see variations page 226

Sweet onions such as Vidalia, if you can find them, make the best onion rings, encased in light crispy batter spiced up with a little chilli powder.

300 g (3½ oz) GF plain flour mix
   (page 16)
110 g (4 oz) cornflour
1½ tsp chilli powder
1 tsp garlic powder

salt
470 ml (16 fl. oz) club soda
3 large onions (sweet onions if possible)
canola oil, for frying

In a large bowl, whisk together the flour mix, cornflour, chilli powder, garlic powder and salt. Whisk in the club soda to make a thick batter.

Peel and slice the onions and separate into rings. Pour oil into a large frying pan to a depth of 8 cm (3 in) and heat until it reaches 190°C (380°F) on a deep-frying thermometer. Dip the onion rings in the batter and let any excess drip off. Gently drop them, in batches, into the oil and fry for 2 minutes on each side, until golden brown. Keep an eye on the temperature of the oil, keeping it at 190°C (380°F) for best frying.

Transfer the onion rings with a slotted spoon to paper towels to drain and keep warm while you cook the rest. Serve as quickly as possible, sprinkled with a little salt.

Serves 6–8

fragrant potato &
cauliflower bhuna

see variations page 227

A bhuna is an Indian dish in which all the spices are first sautéed in oil to bring out their flavour. Spicy but not too hot, this bhuna goes beautifully with chicken korma (page 156).

2 tbsp canola oil
1 large onion, coarsely
    chopped
2 cloves garlic, crushed
2 tsp finely chopped fresh
    root ginger
2 green chillies, finely
    chopped
1 tsp coriander seeds
1 tsp mustard seeds

6 cardamom pods, crushed,
    seeds only
1 tbsp ground turmeric
2 tsp garam masala
1 tbsp soya sauce
2 tbsp brown sugar
2 medium potatoes,
    peeled and cut into
    2.5-cm (1-in) chunks

1 400-g (14-oz) tin chopped
    tomatoes in juice
450 g (1 lb) small cauliflower
    florets
4 tbsp chopped coriander
salt and freshly ground
    black pepper

In a large frying pan, heat the canola oil. When it is hot, but not smoking, add the onion and garlic and cook for 5 minutes, until softened. Add the root ginger, chillies and spices and cook over a medium heat for 5 minutes, to release the flavours. Add the soya sauce, brown sugar, potatoes and tomatoes, cover and cook over a gentle heat for 25 minutes, until the potatoes are slightly tender but still intact.

Add the cauliflower and coriander, cover and cook for a further 20–25 minutes, until the cauliflower is cooked al dente. Season to taste with salt and pepper and serve hot.
Serves 4

sweet potato casserole

see variations page 228

With orange juice, pecans, honey and a little touch of chipotle chilli powder, this sweet potato casserole ticks all the boxes.

4 medium sweet potatoes
1 egg
60 g (2 oz) butter, melted and
    cooled slightly
3 tbsp orange juice
1 tsp vanilla extract

60 g (2 oz) unsalted butter
255 g (9 oz) pecan halves
110 g (4 oz) honey
2 tbsp sugar
1 tsp chipotle chilli powder
230 g (8 oz) mini marshmallows

Grease a 23-cm (9-in) square shallow baking dish and preheat the oven to 175°C (350°F/Gas mark 4). Peel the potatoes and cut them into 5-cm (2-in) chunks. In a large saucepan three-quarters full of water, boil the potatoes for 15–20 minutes, until tender. Drain, return to the pan and mash with a fork. In a medium bowl, beat the egg and add the melted butter, orange juice and vanilla. Beat mixture into the potatoes. Transfer to the baking dish.

In a medium saucepan, melt the unsalted butter, then add the pecans, honey, sugar and chipotle chilli powder. Stirring continuously, cook over a gentle heat for 8–10 minutes, until the butter and sugar caramelise around the nuts. Pour out onto parchment paper to cool.

Spread the marshmallows on the top in a single layer and arrange the caramelised pecans evenly on top. Bake in the oven for 30–35 minutes, until the marshmallows are lightly browned. Turn the heat down if they look like they are browning too fast. Serve hot.

Serves 6

butternut squash & quinoa patties

see variations page 229

Butternut squash is one of the most versatile of all the vegetables. Its flavour blends with quinoa and rice to make these delicious patties. They're a filling side dish or a great vegetarian meal.

1 medium butternut squash
1 tbsp olive oil
230 g (8 oz) quinoa
470 ml (16 fl. oz) water
1 chicken or vegetable stock cube
85 g (3 oz) wild rice

85 g (3 oz) basmati rice
cooking oil spray
110 g (4 oz) finely sliced spring onions
85 g (3 oz) dried cranberries
1 tbsp dried sage
salt and freshly ground black pepper

Preheat the oven to 200°C (400°F/Gas mark 6). Cut the squash in half, remove the seeds and place in a roasting tin. Drizzle with the olive oil and roast in the oven for about an hour or until the squash is tender. Remove from the oven and allow to cool enough to handle. Spoon the flesh out of the skin into a large bowl. Set aside. In a medium saucepan, boil the quinoa in 470 ml (16 fl. oz) water with a chicken stock cube for about 10–12 minutes, until all the water has been absorbed. Remove from the heat, fluff with a fork, cover and set aside for 10 minutes.

Boil a large saucepan three-quarters filled with water. Add the wild rice and basmati rice and cook for 20 minutes. Drain and set aside. Spray a baking tray with a little oil. Mix the quinoa and rice into the butternut squash purée, then mix in the remaining ingredients. Using your hands, form the mixture into burger-size patties. Place them on the baking tray, spray with a little oil and bake 15–20 minutes. Serve hot, warm or cold.
Serves 6

cranberry & pecan baked wild rice with shallots

see variations page 230

Good-quality chicken stock adds depth of flavour to the rice during cooking and the pink cranberries and crunch of pecans add interest.

1 tbsp canola oil
1 tbsp unsalted butter
2 large shallots, finely chopped
170 g (6 oz) long-grain rice
60 g (2 oz) wild rice
600 ml (20 fl. oz) good-quality chicken stock

85 g (3 oz) dried cranberries
1 bay leaf
1/2 tsp dried thyme
salt and freshly ground black pepper
60 g (2 oz) chopped pecans
2 tbsp freshly chopped parsley

Preheat the oven to 190°C (375°F/Gas mark 5).

In a large, heavy flameproof casserole, heat the oil and butter, add the shallots and cook for 5 minutes over a gentle heat, until softened. Add the rices and stir to coat the grains with oil. Stir in the stock, cranberries, bay leaf, thyme, salt and pepper. Bring to the boil, then remove from the heat. Stir, cover and bake in the oven for about 40–45 minutes, until the rice is cooked and tender.

Remove from the oven, stir, discard the bay leaf and taste, adjusting the seasoning if necessary. Stir in the pecans and parsley. Serve hot, warm or cold.

Serves 6

lemon & pea risotto

see variations page 231

This is a lovely fresh, summery risotto, with a subtle lemony tang and faint hint of garlic.

950 ml (32 fl. oz) stock
240 ml (8 fl. oz) white wine
60 g (2 oz) butter
1 small onion, finely chopped
1 clove garlic, crushed
340 g (12 oz) raw Arborio rice

$\frac{1}{2}$ tsp fresh thyme leaves
170 g (6 oz) fresh or frozen peas
zest and juice of 1 lemon
30 g (1 oz) finely shredded Parmesan cheese,
    plus extra to serve
salt and freshly ground black pepper

In a large jug, mix the stock and wine together. In a large saucepan, melt the butter over a medium heat, add the onion and garlic and cook for 5 minutes, until softened. Add the rice and turn it around to coat it with the butter. Stir in the thyme leaves. Keep the heat at medium and add the stock and wine a little at a time. Stir constantly while the liquid is absorbed before adding more. Keep going, stirring constantly, until all the liquid has been added and absorbed and the rice is cooked, but still with a bit of a bite, about 30 minutes in total. Add the peas after 20 minutes of cooking.

Just before serving, add the lemon zest and juice and the Parmesan cheese. Season to taste with salt and pepper and serve immediately with a few Parmesan shavings sprinkled over the top.

Serves 4–6

quinoa & avocado salad with orange dressing

see variations page 232

This appetising make-ahead salad is so colourful that it will tempt even the most fussy family member.

for the orange dressing
90 ml (3 fl. oz) extra-virgin olive oil
3 tbsp white wine vinegar
2 tbsp juice drained from the
    mandarin oranges
2 tsp Dijon mustard
2 tsp lime juice
salt and freshly ground black pepper

for the salad
470 ml (16 fl. oz) water
230 g (8 oz) quinoa
1 310-g (11-oz) tin mandarin oranges
110 g (4 oz) seeded and diced yellow
    pepper
60 g (2 oz) dried cherries
4 spring onions, finely sliced
1 avocado, peeled, pitted and diced
60 g (2 oz) chopped pecans
3 tbsp freshly chopped parsley

In a medium jug, whisk the dressing ingredients together and set aside. In a large saucepan, bring the water to a boil. Add the quinoa and simmer gently for 10–12 minutes, until all the water has been absorbed. Remove from the heat, fluff with a fork, cover and set aside for 10 minutes. Transfer to a large bowl and set aside to cool for 10 minutes. Drain the rest of the juice from the mandarin oranges and add the oranges to the quinoa. Stir in the yellow pepper, dried cherries and spring onions. Cover and chill until required. Just before serving, add the avocado, chopped pecans and parsley. Serve with the orange dressing.

Serves 4

mixed tomato salad with pomegranate treacle dressing

see variations page 233

Tomatoes love sugar, so the sweetness of the pomegranate treacle in the dressing brings out their flavour beautifully. Find a nice assortment of tomato colours (a farmers' market is a good place to look).

for the dressing
355 ml (12 fl. oz) pomegranate juice
2 tsp lemon juice
2 tbsp sugar
2 tbsp extra-virgin olive oil
2 shallots, finely chopped

for the salad
700 g (1½ lbs) small tomatoes (in assorted colours, if possible)
60 g (2 oz) crumbled feta cheese
3 tbsp freshly chopped coriander, plus extra to serve
40 g (1½ oz) pomegranate seeds

To make pomegranate treacle, in a medium saucepan, over a medium heat, simmer together the pomegranate juice, lemon juice and sugar until the liquid is thick and syrupy and has reduced to about 90 ml (3 fl. oz). Set aside to cool. Make the dressing by whisking together the cooled pomegranate treacle, olive oil and shallots.

Just before serving, mix together the tomatoes, feta cheese and coriander in a serving bowl. Fold in the dressing. Sprinkle a little extra coriander and the pomegranate seeds over the top. Serve immediately.

Serves 4

potato dauphinois with garlic & swiss cheese

see variations page 234

Potatoes are layered with swiss cheese, onion and garlic and baked until the flavours are blended together and the top is golden brown.

2 tbsp (1 oz) butter, plus extra for greasing
900 g (2 lbs) potatoes
1 large onion, finely chopped
2 cloves garlic, finely chopped
230 g (8 oz) finely shredded swiss cheese
salt and freshly ground black pepper
240 ml (8 fl. oz) single cream

Grease a large ovenproof casserole dish with a little butter. Preheat the oven to 190°C (375°F/Gas mark 5).

Peel and finely slice the potatoes. Put a layer, overlapping, in the bottom of the dish, dot with butter, sprinkle with some of the onion, garlic and cheese and season with salt and pepper. Pour in about 60 ml (2 fl. oz) of the single cream. Repeat the layers until all the ingredients have been used up, finishing with a layer of cheese and pouring the last of the single cream over the top.

Cover and bake in the oven for at least 1 hour or until the potatoes are tender when pierced with a skewer. If the top is not sufficiently golden brown, finish it off under a hot grill for 5 minutes.

Serves 4

pilau rice

see variations page 235

The perfect accompaniment to dishes with a lot of sauce, try this rice with the chicken korma (page 156).

340 g (12 oz) basmati rice	pinch saffron
1 tbsp (¹/₂ oz) butter	1 bay leaf
1 small onion, finely chopped	salt and freshly ground black pepper
2 cardamom pods	300 ml (10 fl. oz) hot chicken stock
¹/₂ tsp ground cumin	handful sliced almonds, toasted
¹/₂ tsp ground cinnamon	freshly chopped coriander, to serve

Under cold water, wash and drain the rice. In a medium saucepan, melt the butter and cook the onion over a gentle heat for about 10 minutes or until softened and slightly golden. Add the spices, saffron, bay leaf, salt and pepper and cook for 5 minutes. Add the rice to the pan, stir to coat it in the butter and add the stock. Mix well, cover the saucepan first with aluminium foil and then with a lid, so that it is really sealed. Cook very gently for 10 minutes, then turn off the heat and leave for a further 5 minutes without removing the covers.

To serve, fluff the rice with a fork and serve sprinkled with toasted sliced almonds and freshly chopped coriander.

Serves 4

variations

stuffed peppers

see base recipe page 197

stuffed peppers with minced lamb & cumin
Prepare the basic recipe, omitting half the rice and replacing with 230 g
(8 oz) raw ground lamb. Add 1 teaspoon ground cumin and 1 teaspoon
ground coriander to the stuffing mixture.

stuffed peppers with squash & swiss cheese
Prepare the basic recipe, replacing half the rice with 230 g (8 oz) diced
butternut squash and 110 g (4 oz) finely shredded swiss cheese.

stuffed peppers with courgette
Prepare the basic recipe, adding 110 g (4 oz) diced courgette to the mixture.

stuffed peppers with red kidney beans & chilli
Prepare the basic recipe, replacing 85 g (3 oz) of the rice with 170 g
(6 oz) drained tinned red kidney beans. Add 1 teaspoon chilli powder to
the mixture.

spicy potato wedges with soured cream dip

see base recipe page 198

sweet & spicy potato wedges with soured cream dip
Prepare the basic recipe, replacing the potatoes with sweet potatoes.

rosemary roasted potatoes
Prepare the basic recipe, replacing half the potatoes with sweet potatoes. Cut into 1.3-cm (½-in) cubes and sprinkle with dried rosemary in place of the Cajun seasoning.

casey's potatoes with peppers
Instead of the basic recipe, cut the potatoes into 0.6-cm (¼-in) cubes. In a large bowl, mix with 1 finely chopped small onion, 1 seeded and finely chopped green pepper, 20 g (¾ oz) white rice flour, pinch paprika, 2 tablespoons freshly chopped parsley, 60 g (2 oz) finely shredded Cheddar cheese and salt and freshly ground black pepper. Transfer to a greased casserole dish, pour over 120 ml (4 fl. oz) each of hot milk and thick cream and bake at 200°C (400°F/Gas mark 6) for 1 hour or until the potatoes are cooked through.

dairy-free spicy potato wedges with honey–mustard mayo
Prepare the basic recipe, replacing the butter with olive oil and the soured cream with 5 tablespoons good-quality mayonnaise mixed with 1 tablespoon Dijon mustard and 1 tablespoon honey.

green bean casserole with garlic & walnuts

see base recipe page 200

green bean casserole with garlic, walnuts & pine nuts
Prepare the basic recipe, adding 85 g (3 oz) pine nuts to the green beans before pouring in the sauce.

green bean casserole with garlic, walnuts & cheese sauce
Prepare the basic recipe, omitting the mushrooms and substituting 110 g (4 oz) finely shredded Cheddar cheese and 1 teaspoon Dijon mustard.

green bean casserole with tomatoes & spinach
Prepare the basic recipe, omitting the mushrooms and substituting 110 g (4 oz) finely shredded Cheddar cheese and 1 teaspoon Dijon mustard. Add 1 skinned, seeded and chopped tomato and 30 g (1 oz) fresh spinach leaves to the beans in the casserole before pouring in the sauce. Omit the walnuts.

dairy-free green bean casserole with garlic & walnuts
Prepare the basic recipe, replacing the butter with dairy-free margarine and the milk with rice milk. Omit the Parmesan cheese.

aubergine, tomato & courgette casserole

see base recipe page 203

aubergine, tomato & courgette casserole with shallots
Prepare the basic recipe, adding 3 finely chopped shallots to the layers.

aubergine, tomato & courgette casserole with chillies
Prepare the basic recipe, adding 2 finely chopped mild chillies to the layers.

aubergine & courgette casserole with cheese & chives
Prepare the basic recipe, adding 60 g (2 oz) shredded Cheddar cheese to the layers and replacing the rosemary with chopped chives. Top with the Parmesan cheese.

mixed vegetable casserole with basil & peppers
Prepare the basic recipe, replacing 2 courgettes with 2 seeded and sliced green peppers and the rosemary with 40 g (1½ oz) freshly chopped basil.

variations

crispy onion rings

see base recipe page 204

crispy onion rings with chilli dipping sauce
Prepare the basic recipe and serve with chilli sauce made by mixing
3 tablespoons sweet chilli sauce with 3 tablespoons tomato ketchup and
3 tablespoons medium–hot salsa.

crispy courgette strips
Prepare the basic recipe, replacing the onions with 4–5 courgettes, sliced
into strips.

crispy carrot sticks
Prepare the basic recipe, replacing the onions with 3–4 carrots, peeled and
sliced into sticks.

crispy onion rings with creamy remoulade dipping sauce
Prepare the basic recipe. Stir together 110 g (4 oz) mayonnaise,
2 teaspoons tomato ketchup, 2 teaspoons creamed horseradish,
$\frac{1}{4}$ teaspoon paprika, $\frac{1}{8}$ teaspoon each of garlic powder and dried
oregano and a pinch of salt, pepper and cayenne pepper.

fragrant potato & cauliflower bhuna

see base recipe page 207

fragrant sweet potato & cauliflower bhuna
Prepare the basic recipe, replacing the potatoes with sweet potatoes.

fragrant potato & cauliflower bhuna with peppers
Prepare the basic recipe, adding 1 red pepper, seeded and sliced, to the
frying pan with the onion.

bombay aloo
Prepare the basic recipe, omitting the cauliflower and adding 3 more
medium potatoes.

fragrant butternut squash & cauliflower bhuna
Prepare the basic recipe, omitting the potatoes and substituting 450 g (1 lb)
peeled and diced butternut squash.

mixed vegetable bhuna
Prepare the basic recipe, using a selection of vegetables, such as carrots,
courgettes, cauliflower, sweet potatoes, peas and corn. If the sauce is too
runny, thicken it with 2 teaspoons cornflour mixed to a paste with a
little water.

variations

sweet potato casserole

see base recipe page 208

sweet potato casserole with streusel topping
Prepare the basic recipe omitting the pecan topping and marshmallows.
Mix 110 g (4 oz) brown sugar with 40 g (1½ oz) white rice flour and cut in
60 g (2 oz) butter until it resembles breadcrumbs. Stir in 85 g (3 oz)
chopped pecans and spread over the top of the sweet potatoes. Bake for
25–30 minutes.

sweet potato casserole with meringue topping
Prepare the basic recipe, omitting the pecan topping and marshmallows.
In a medium bowl, whisk 2 egg whites until soft peaks form. Gradually whisk
in 60 g (2 oz) caster sugar, beating until stiff. Place in a piping bag with a
large nozzle and pipe small peaks on the sweet potatoes. Bake for 25–30
minutes, until the meringue has lightly browned and crisped.

sweet potato casserole with coconut
Prepare the basic recipe, adding 40 g (1½ oz) shredded coconut to the sweet
potato and egg mixture.

dairy-free sweet potato casserole
Prepare the basic recipe, replacing the butter with dairy-free margarine in
both the sweet potato and the caramelised pecans.

variations

butternut squash & quinoa patties

see base recipe page 211

butternut squash & quinoa patties with bacon
Prepare the basic recipe. Add 4 strips of bacon, cooked until crisp and crumbled, to the mixture.

butternut squash & quinoa patties with chilli & coriander
Prepare the basic recipe, omitting the sage. Add 2 green chillies and 30 g (1 oz) freshly chopped coriander to the mixture.

sweet potato & quinoa patties
Prepare the basic recipe, replacing the butternut squash with mashed sweet potatoes. Peel and cut 2 large sweet potatoes into chunks. Boil for 20 minutes until tender and mash.

butternut squash & quinoa patties with parmesan & basil
Prepare the basic recipe, replacing the sage with 30 g (1 oz) freshly chopped basil. Add 2 tablespoons finely shredded Parmesan cheese to the mixture.

potato & quinoa patties with cabbage
Prepare the basic recipe, replacing the squash, wild rice and rice with 3 cooked, mashed large potatoes and 450 g (1 lb) cooked green cabbage.

variations

cranberry & pecan baked wild rice with shallots

see base recipe page 212

cherry & walnut baked orzo with shallots
Prepare the basic recipe, replacing the wild rice and rice with orzo, the cranberries with dried cherries and the pecans with walnuts.

cranberry & pecan baked jasmine rice with whole kernel corn
Prepare the basic recipe, replacing both rices with jasmine rice. Add 170 g (6 oz) drained whole kernel corn 10 minutes before the end of cooking time.

cranberry & pecan baked wild rice with celery & chives
Prepare the basic recipe, adding 2 finely chopped celery stalks to the pan with the stock. Replace the parsley with chives.

cranberry & pecan baked wild rice with peas & parmesan
Prepare the basic recipe, adding 170 g (6 oz) fresh or frozen peas 20 minutes before the end of cooking time. Add 30 g (1 oz) finely shredded Parmesan cheese with the parsley.

dairy-free wild rice with leeks & spinach
Prepare the basic recipe, replacing the butter with dairy-free margarine. Add 1 finely chopped leek to the pan with the shallots and add 60 g (2 oz) fresh spinach leaves 15 minutes before the end of cooking time.

lemon & pea risotto

see base recipe page 214

lemon & courgette risotto
Prepare the basic recipe, omitting the peas and substituting 1 finely
chopped courgette.

lemon, leek & sage risotto
Prepare the basic recipe, omitting the peas. Add 1 finely chopped leek to the pan with
the onion. Replace the thyme leaves with 2 teaspoons dried sage.

sun-dried tomato & basil risotto
Prepare the basic recipe, omitting the thyme and adding 70 g (2½ oz) chopped sun-dried
tomatoes and 40 g (1½ oz) freshly chopped basil with the Parmesan cheese.

roasted squash & saffron risotto
Prepare the basic recipe, omitting the peas. Roast 230 g (8 oz) peeled, seeded and cubed
butternut squash, drizzled with oil, at 200°C (400°F/Gas mark 6) for 20 minutes and add
to the risotto with the Parmesan cheese. Add a few saffron threads with the rice.

dairy-free lemon, asparagus & mint risotto
Prepare the basic recipe, replacing the butter with olive oil, the thyme with 2 teaspoons
freshly chopped mint and the peas with asparagus spears.

variations

quinoa & avocado salad with orange dressing

see base recipe page 217

quinoa & avocado salad with cranberries
Prepare the basic recipe, replacing the cherries with dried cranberries.

quinoa & apple salad with honey-mustard dressing
Prepare the basic recipe, omitting the avocado and mandarin oranges in
the salad and substituting 1 peeled, cored and diced apple, such as Golden
Delicious. Omit the orange juice in the dressing and add 1 tablespoon honey
to the dressing during whisking.

brown rice & celery salad with asian dressing
Prepare the basic recipe, replacing the quinoa with 510 g (18 oz)
cooked brown rice. Replace the orange dressing with an Asian
dressing. Whisk together 4 tablespoons soya sauce, 2 tablespoons Dijon
mustard, ½ teaspoon sesame oil, ½ teaspoon minced root ginger and
2 tablespoons water.

mixed tomato salad with pomegranate treacle dressing

see base recipe page 218

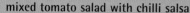

mixed tomato salad with chilli salsa

Prepare the basic recipe, omitting the dressing and pomegranate seeds. Make chilli salsa by mixing 1 small finely chopped red onion, 1 minced garlic clove, 30 g (1 oz) freshly chopped coriander, 1 teaspoon extra-virgin olive oil, 1 teaspoon lime juice, 1 finely chopped red chilli and salt and pepper. Serve over the tomato salad.

mixed tomato & basil salad with vinaigrette

Prepare the basic recipe, omitting the pomegranate seeds and replacing the coriander with basil. Replace the dressing with a vinaigrette. Mix together 60 ml (2 fl. oz) extra-virgin olive oil, 1 tablespoon red wine vinegar, 1 finely chopped small shallot and salt and freshly ground black pepper.

mixed tomato & snow pea salad with garlic vinaigrette

Prepare the basic recipe, omitting the pomegranate seeds, adding 85 g (3 oz) chopped snow peas to the salad. Serve with the vinaigrette from variation above, with 1 finely chopped clove garlic added and using coriander instead of basil.

variations

potato dauphinois with garlic & swiss cheese

see base recipe page 220

potato dauphinois with cheddar cheese
Prepare the basic recipe, replacing the single cream with milk and the swiss cheese with Cheddar cheese.

potato dauphinois with tomatoes
Prepare the basic recipe, adding 4 skinned, seeded and chopped tomatoes to the layers and 2 tablespoons freshly chopped parsley to the layers.

potato dauphinois with whole kernel corn
Prepare the basic recipe, adding 170 g (6 oz) drained whole kernel corn to the layers.

potato dauphinois with ham
Prepare the basic recipe, adding 230 g (8 oz) thinly sliced ham with the layers.

dairy-free potatoes boulangère
Prepare the basic recipe, replacing the butter for greasing with oil and the butter and single cream with good-quality chicken or vegetable stock. Omit the cheese.

variations

pilau rice

see base recipe page 221

spanish rice
Prepare basic recipe, omitting cardomom pods and cumin. Add 1 sliced red pepper and 2 crushed garlic cloves with the onion. Stir through 40 g (1½ oz) pitted and chopped black olives when fluffing the rice.

thai coconut rice
Prepare basic recipe, omitting cardomom pods and cumin. Add 1 tablespoon red Thai curry paste with the stock and stir in 30 g (1 oz) unsweetened shredded coconut and 40 g (1½ oz) freshly chopped coriander.

moroccan rice with mushrooms & parsley
Prepare basic recipe, adding 2 crushed garlic cloves and 110 g (4 oz) chopped mushrooms with the onion. Before serving, stir in the zest of 1 lemon and 40 g (1½ oz) freshly chopped parsley.

dairy-free pilau rice with chickpeas & spinach
Prepare basic recipe, replacing butter with canola oil. Heat 1 400-g (14-oz) tin chickpeas with 60 g (2 oz) fresh spinach, drain and add to the rice before serving.

desserts

In this chapter you will find treats and indulgences

to thrill even the most discerning guest or family

member. Gluten will definitely not be missed!

orange & polenta cake

see variations page 268

Polenta or fine cornmeal, makes a great base for a cake. Add oranges to the mixture and serve warm with ice cream and you have a delicious dessert.

170 g (6 oz) unsalted butter, softened
170 g (6 oz) sugar
4 large eggs
230 g (8 oz) ground almonds
110 g (4 oz) fine polenta (fine cornmeal)
60 g (2 oz) rice flour

2 tsp baking powder
$\frac{1}{2}$ tsp xantham gum
$\frac{1}{2}$ tsp salt
zest and juice of 2 oranges
caster sugar, to serve

Grease a round 20-cm (9-in) cake tin and line the base and sides with parchment paper. Preheat the oven to 160°C (325°F/Gas mark 3).

In a large bowl, cream the butter and sugar together until light and fluffy. Add the eggs, a little at a time, beating well after each addition. In a large bowl, whisk together the ground almonds, polenta, rice flour, baking powder, xantham gum and salt and add to the butter mixture with the orange zest and juice. Transfer the mixture to the cake tin, smooth the top with a palette knife and bake for about 45 minutes or until a cocktail stick inserted into the centre of the cake comes out clean.

Remove from the oven, remove cake from tin and allow to cool completely on a wire rack. Sprinkle a little caster sugar on the top of the cake and serve warm or cold.

Makes 1 cake

hazelnut meringue cake with raspberry coulis

see variations page 269

This is ideal for special occasions and if you fill the meringue at least 3 hours before serving, the cake will cut without splintering.

90 g (3 oz) hazelnuts, shelled
4 egg whites
300 g (10 oz) granulated sugar
2 tsp vanilla extract, divided
$^1\!/_2$ tsp white wine vinegar
355 ml (12 fl. oz) thick cream

60 g (2 oz) caster sugar
230 g (8 oz) fresh raspberries for coulis
110 g (4 oz) fresh raspberries for filling
4 tbsp icing sugar, plus extra
    for dusting

Grease and flour the base and sides of 2 20-cm (8-in) cake tins and line the base with nonstick parchment paper. Preheat the oven to 190°C (375°F/Gas mark 5). In a small frying pan, brown the hazelnuts over a medium heat. Allow to cool, then place in a food processor and pulse until ground. Transfer to a small bowl and set aside to cool completely.

In a spotlessly clean, large bowl, whisk the egg whites, preferably by hand with a balloon whisk, which gives a greater volume. You can also use an electric whisk. When the egg whites are forming soft peaks, add the granulated sugar 1 tablespoon at a time and whisk until the mixture is very stiff. Whisk in 1 teaspoon vanilla extract, the vinegar and the ground nuts. Divide the mixture between the cake tins and smooth the top gently with a palette knife. Bake in the oven for 30–40 minutes. Turn out onto a wire rack to cool.

To make the coulis, rub the raspberries through a nylon sieve into a small bowl, then beat in the icing sugar 1 tablespoon at a time. Place in a serving jug, cover and chill until required. In a bowl, whip the cream, add remaining vanilla extract and sweeten with the caster sugar. Place 1 cake upside down on a serving plate, spread with two-thirds of the whipped cream and sprinkle with raspberries. Place the other cake, right side up, on top.

Dust the cake with icing sugar and use the rest of the whipped cream to decorate the top. To serve, drizzle each portion with a little raspberry coulis.

Serves 6

carrot & pineapple cake with cream cheese frosting

see variations page 270

Moist and luscious, carrot cake is always a favourite. Now you can enjoy it even on a gluten-free diet. The pineapple adds a tropical touch.

120 ml (4 fl. oz) canola oil
110 g (4 oz) sugar
110 g (4 oz) brown sugar
3 eggs
2 tbsp orange juice
130 g (4½ oz) cornflour
90 g (3¼ oz) potato starch
30 g (1 oz) rice flour
1 tsp bicarbonate of soda
1 tsp baking powder
2 tsp ground cinnamon
1 tsp ground nutmeg

1 tsp ground ginger
½ tsp salt
1 tsp xantham gum
40 g (1½ oz) chopped pecans
40 g (1½ oz) drained crushed pineapple
3 large carrots, finely shredded

for the frosting
110 g (4 oz) unsalted butter, room temperature
230 g (8 oz) cream cheese, room temperature
pinch salt
450 g (1 lb) icing sugar, sifted
1 tsp vanilla extract

Grease 2 round 20-cm (8-in) cake tins with a little oil and line the bases with parchment paper. Preheat the oven to 160°C (325°F/Gas mark 3). In a large bowl, whisk together the oil, sugar, brown sugar, eggs and orange juice. In another large bowl, whisk together the cornflour, potato starch, rice flour, bicarbonate of soda, baking powder, spices, salt and xantham gum. Make a well in the centre and pour in the wet ingredients. Stir in the pecans, pineapple and shredded carrots. Mix well and divide between the cake tins. Smooth the tops with a palette knife.

Bake for about 40–45 minutes or until a cocktail stick inserted into the cakes comes out clean. Remove from the oven, turn out onto wire racks and allow to cool completely.

Make frosting by creaming together the butter, cream cheese and salt. Gradually add the icing sugar and vanilla and beat until light and fluffy. Sandwich the cakes together with frosting, then spread frosting across the top and sides. Chilled until ready to serve.
Makes 1 cake

blueberry & lemon sponge dessert

see variations page 271

Blueberries nestling in a vanilla-infused sponge and dusted with icing sugar, make a delicious coffee cake or dessert with cream or ice cream.

110 g (4 oz) unsalted butter
110 g (4 oz) caster or granulated sugar
2 eggs, lightly beaten
zest of 1 lemon
1 tsp vanilla extract

1 tsp glycerine
230 g (8 oz) GF self-raising flour mix (page 15)
4 tbsp milk (or less)
110 g (4 oz) blueberries

Grease a 20x20-cm (8x8-in) square baking tin and preheat the oven to 175°C (350°F/Gas mark 4).

In a large bowl, using an electric mixer, beat the butter and sugar together until light and creamy. Slowly add the eggs, beating after each addition, then beat in the lemon zest, vanilla extract and glycerine. Fold in the flour mix, adding just enough of the milk to make a dropping consistency.

Gently fold in the blueberries and transfer to the baking tin, smoothing the top. Bake in the oven for 30 minutes, until risen and golden brown. Serve hot, warm or cold.

Serves 9

chocolate & cherry roulade

see variations page 272

With its rich chocolate flavour and sweetened whipped cream and cherry filling, this is excellent for an elegant dinner party or to impress friends for coffee. Start it the day before.

170 g (6 oz) bitter chocolate, broken into pieces
3 tbsp water
4 eggs, separated
170 g (6 oz) granulated sugar, divided

30 g (1 oz) sifted icing sugar
355 ml (12 fl. oz) whipping cream, whipped
170 g (6 oz) pitted cherries

Grease a shallow, 20x30-cm (8x12-in) baking tin and line the base with parchment paper. Preheat the oven to 175°C (350°F/Gas mark 4). In a small tin, heat the chocolate and water very gently until the chocolate has just melted. Set aside to cool slightly. In a medium bowl, whisk the egg yolks with half the granulated sugar until thick and creamy and then whisk in the warm chocolate.

In a large, spotlessly clean bowl, whisk the egg whites until stiff and continue to whisk while you gradually add the remaining granulated sugar. Fold gently into the chocolate mixture. Transfer to the baking tin and bake for 25–30 minutes, until firm. Remove from the oven and leave in the tin to cool for 5 minutes and then cover with a clean damp cloth and chill overnight in the fridge. Carefully remove the cloth and turn the roulade onto a sheet of parchment paper thickly dusted with icing sugar. Peel off the lining paper. Spread three-quarters of the whipped cream evenly over the roulade, sprinkle with cherries and roll up like a jelly roll. Serve immediately or chill until required.

Serves 8

strawberry jam roly-poly

see variations page 273

This is a traditional British pastry dessert, filled with good-quality strawberry jam and rolled up like a jam roll. Serve hot with cream or ice cream.

140 g (5 oz) rice flour, plus extra for rolling
60 g (2 oz) tapioca flour
3 tbsp (1 oz) potato starch
1 tsp baking powder
70 g (2½ oz) sugar
110 g (4 oz) unsalted butter,
    frozen and grated

6–8 tbsp water
8 tbsp good-quality strawberry jam
icing sugar, cream or ice cream,
    to serve

In a large bowl, whisk together the rice flour, tapioca flour, potato starch and baking powder. Add the sugar and grated butter and stir lightly with a fork. Add enough water to make a soft dough. Gather it into a ball with your fingers and sprinkle with rice flour. Place a sheet of clingfilm on the worktop, sprinkle it with rice flour and place the dough on top.

Gently roll out into a 20x27-cm (8x11-in) rectangle. Spread with strawberry jam, leaving a 2.5-cm (1-in) border all around. Using your fingers, lightly dampen the border with a little cold water. Carefully roll up from the long edge farthest from you, using the clingfilm to pull the pastry towards you, making a tubular shape. Press gently to seal the edges. Lightly grease a sheet of parchment paper and lift the roly-poly onto it, using the clingfilm to lift with. The dough is very delicate and will fall apart easily. Tightly roll up in the parchment paper and secure the ends with staples.

Place on a baking tray and bake for 40–45 minutes, until golden brown. Remove from the oven, unwrap, cut into 6 slices and serve immediately, with cream or ice cream and sprinkled with icing sugar.

Serves 6

strawberry shortcake cheesecake

see variations page 274

This is a creamy New York-style cheesecake, topped with a layer of strawberries and a strawberry glaze and decorated with whipped cream. Start the day before.

110 g (4 oz) unsalted
butter, softened
110 g (4 oz) sugar
1 egg
1 tsp almond extract
240 g (8½ oz) GF biscuit flour
mix (page 16)

½ tsp baking powder
60 g (2 oz) sliced almonds
900 g (2 lbs) cream cheese
230 g (8 oz) sugar
4 eggs
1 tsp rice flour
1 tsp vanilla extract

230 g (8 oz) soured cream
230 g (8 oz) strawberries,
hulled and well drained
4 tbsp strawberry jam
300 ml (10 fl. oz)
thick cream, whipped

Generously grease the sides and base of a 26-cm (10-in) springform tin. Preheat the oven to 160°C (325°F/Gas mark 3). In a large bowl, cream together the butter and sugar until light and fluffy. Beat in the egg and almond extract and stir in the biscuit mix and baking powder. Form into a circle shape and pat into the bottom of the tin. Sprinkle the dough with sliced almonds. Set aside. In a large bowl, using an electric mixer, combine the cream cheese, sugar, eggs and rice flour. Beat until smooth. Mix in the vanilla extract and soured cream until just blended. Pour into the tin on top of the shortcake base. Bake for 60 minutes. Turn off the oven and open the door slightly. Leave the cheesecake in the oven for 30 minutes to cool. Remove from the oven and refrigerate, preferably overnight. Cut the strawberries lengthwise in half and arrange them in circles on top of the cheesecake. In a small pan, over a low heat, warm the jam until runny and brush on top of the strawberries to glaze. Using a piping bag and large fluted nozzle, pipe cream rosettes around the edge of the cheesecake to decorate. Chill until required.

Makes 1 26-cm (10-in) cheesecake

french apple flan

see variations page 275

This is a very impressive dessert to serve at special occasions and amazingly delicious, especially with a dollop of whipped cream.

1 23-cm (9-in) GF pastry crust (page 17)

for the filling
900 g (2 lbs) cooking apples
60 g (2 oz) unsalted butter
170 g (6 oz) sugar

for the topping
3–4 sweet eating apples
2 tbsp lemon juice
2 tbsp sugar, to sprinkle
4 tbsp apricot jam, for glaze
whipped cream, to serve

Preheat the oven to 200°C (400°F/Gas mark 6). Follow the instructions for making and partially baking the pastry on page 17.

To make the filling, peel, core and slice the cooking apples. In a large pan, melt the butter and add the apples and sugar. Cover and cook gently for 20–25 minutes, until the apples are soft and fluffy. Set aside to cool. Beat with a wooden spoon until smooth and spread evenly over the part-baked crust.

For the topping, peel, core and quarter the eating apples, then cut into thin slices. Toss in lemon juice and arrange in circles on top of the filling. Sprinkle with sugar and bake for 30–35 minutes until both pastry and apples are light golden in colour. Allow to cool for 10 minutes. Warm the apricot jam, push it through a sieve into a bowl and brush carefully over the apples to glaze. Serve flan warm, with whipped cream.

Serves 8

sweet potato pie with toffee pecan sauce

see variations page 276

Sweet potatoes are amazingly versatile. Their appeal is never-ending, especially when used to fill sweet pastry crust and topped with pecans bathed in a creamy toffee-flavoured topping.

560 g (1¼ lbs) sweet potatoes
1 23-cm (9-in) GF pastry crust (page 17)
1 tsp orange zest
85 g (3 oz) brown sugar
2 tsp pumpkin pie spice
2 eggs, lightly beaten
470 ml (16 fl. oz) whipping cream
3 tbsp brandy or orange juice

for the toffee pecan sauce
2 tbsp (1 oz) unsalted butter
85 g (3 oz) brown sugar
5 tbsp whipping cream
170 g (6 oz) pecan halves
icing sugar, to serve

Preheat the oven to 200°C (400°F/Gas mark 6). Peel the sweet potatoes and cut into 5-cm (2-in) chunks. Three-quarters fill a large pan with water, add the potatoes and bring to the boil. Simmer for about 30 minutes or until the potatoes are very tender. Drain well and press through a sieve. Set aside the purée in a large bowl to cool. While the potatoes are cooking, prepare and partially bake the pastry, as directed on page 17. Once the potato purée has cooled, add the orange zest, brown sugar and pumpkin pie spice. Stir in the beaten eggs and mix well. Gradually add the cream and brandy or orange juice, stirring continuously and carefully pour into the crust. Bake for about 40 minutes, until just set. The centre should still

be a little wobbly. Set aside to cool slightly. To make the topping, in a small tin, heat the butter and brown sugar, stirring continuously, until the sugar has dissolved. Add the cream and simmer for 4 minutes or until bubbling and slightly thickened.

Remove from the heat, stir in the pecans and allow to cool slightly. Spoon over the pie. Serve pie slightly warm or cooled, dusted with icing sugar.

Serves 8

profiteroles with chocolate sauce

see variations page 277

These little rounds of choux pastry (often referred to as a cream puff) are crisp on the outside, filled with light and fluffy whipped cream and smothered in fudgy chocolate sauce.

90 g (3 oz) rice flour
40 g (1½ oz)
    potato starch
½ tsp salt
½ tsp baking powder
70 g (2½ oz)
    unsalted butter

240 ml (8 fl. oz) full-fat milk
3 large eggs
180 ml (6 fl. oz) thick cream

for the chocolate sauce
1 140-g (5-oz) tin evaporated
    milk

60 g (2 oz) plain chocolate
60 g (2 oz) brown sugar
icing sugar, to serve

Line a baking tray with parchment paper and preheat the oven to 190°C (375°F/Gas mark 5). In a small bowl, mix together the rice flour, potato starch, salt and baking powder. In a medium saucepan, over a medium heat, combine the butter and milk and bring to the boil. Add the flour mixture and stir vigorously until the mixture pulls away from the side of the tin. Beat in eggs, one at a time, until incorporated. Transfer to a piping bag with a fluted or plain nozzle and pipe small balls (just over an inch round) onto the parchment paper, leaving room for them to rise. Bake in the oven for 10–15 minutes until puffed and golden.

Remove from the oven and transfer to a wire rack to cool. Make a small slit low down in the side of each profiterole. Whip the thick cream, spoon into a piping bag with a small nozzle and pipe a little of the cream into each choux bun. Chill until ready to serve. Meanwhile, make the chocolate sauce.

In a small pan, heat the evaporated milk with the chocolate and brown sugar over a low heat until the sugar has dissolved. Bring to the boil, then simmer gently for 3 minutes. Set aside to cool slightly. Arrange the profiteroles into a pyramid shape on a large serving plate, placing them on top of each other. If you have any whipped cream left over, pipe small cream rosettes between the profiteroles and dust the pyramid with icing sugar. Pour the chocolate sauce over the top so that it trickles down the side and serve the rest of the sauce separately.

Serves 4

lemon mousse

see variations page 278

Light and creamy, this is a wonderful fresh dessert at the end of a rich meal.

4 tsp unflavoured gelatin
3–4 tbsp water
6 large eggs, separated
230 g (8 oz) sugar
juice and finely shredded rind of 3 lemons

300 ml (10 fl. oz) whipping cream
180 ml (6 fl. oz) thick cream, to serve
grated chocolate, to serve

In a medium bowl, soak the gelatin in the water and leave until soft. In a large bowl, whisk the egg yolks and sugar together until light, pale and fluffy. Add the lemon juice, lemon rind and whipping cream and whisk again.

In a small saucepan, bring 2 in of water to the boil, then remove it from the heat. Place the bowl of gelatin over the water, not in it and let dissolve slowly. When it has turned stringy, add to the lemon mixture.

In a large, spotlessly clean bowl, whisk the egg whites until stiff peaks form. Gently fold into the lemon mixture and stir until just combined. Transfer to a serving bowl and chill in the fridge until set, preferably overnight.

Before serving, whip the thick cream until soft peaks form. Either pipe the cream in whirls over the top of the mousse or spread the cream over the surface. Sprinkle the top with a little grated chocolate.

Serves 6

marsala poached peaches & mascarpone cream

see variations page 279

Poached in marsala and chilled until very cold, peaches become succulent and delicious. Serve with mascarpone and fromage frais and you have a dessert made in heaven.

4 firm but ripe peaches
240 ml (8 fl. oz) sweet marsala wine
2 tbsp amaretto liqueur
4 tbsp sugar
2 tbsp honey

1 tsp cornflour mixed with 2 tsp water
4 tbsp Italian mascarpone, room temperature
4 tbsp fromage frais
3 tbsp honey

Preheat the oven to 160°C (325°F/Gas mark 3). Halve the peaches, remove the pits and place the peaches in a large bowl. Cover with boiling water, leave for 1 minute, drain and slide the skins off. Place them in a shallow baking dish. In a medium bowl, mix the marsala with the amaretto, sugar and honey. Pour mixture over the peaches. Bake, uncovered, for 25–30 minutes. Remove from the oven and set aside to cool for 10 minutes.

Place the peaches In a serving dish, cover and place in the refrigerator. Pour the wine and sugar syrup from the baking dish into a small saucepan. Bring to the boil. Mix the dissolved cornflour into the syrup, stirring, until it thickens. Set aside to cool and then pour over the peaches. Chill until really cold, about 6 hours. In a medium bowl, mix the mascarpone, fromage frais and honey until combined. Cover and chill until required. Serve 2 peach halves per person, with the sauce spooned over and mascarpone cream on the side.

Serves 4

chocolate-covered praline ice cream balls

see variations page 280

Praline is mixed into homemade ice cream and covered in chocolate. This dessert looks impressive, but is surprisingly easy to make.

3 egg yolks
170 g (6 oz) sugar
300 ml (10 fl. oz)
    single cream
2 tbsp instant coffee powder

300 ml (10 fl. oz) thick cream,
    whipped
110 g (4 oz) caster sugar
85 g (3 oz) whole unblanched
    almonds

170 g (6 oz) plain chocolate
    morsels, melted and cooled
chocolate sauce (page 254)

Lightly oil a baking tray with vegetable oil and line another sheet with aluminium foil. In a large bowl, beat the egg yolks and sugar together until creamy. In a medium pan, bring the single cream and instant coffee powder to the boil, pour onto the egg yolks and beat until mixed thoroughly. Transfer mixture to the top of a double boiler or a heatproof bowl over a tin of hot water and cook, stirring continuously, until thick enough to coat the back of the spoon. Strain through a sieve into a bowl and set aside to cool. Fold into the whipped cream, transfer to a rigid freezer container, cover and freeze for about 2 hours.

To make the praline, place the caster sugar and almonds in a small heavy-based pan and heat until the sugar caramelises and the almonds begin to split. Turn out onto the oiled baking tray and set aside until cool. Crush the cooled praline in a food processor until finely ground. Remove the ice cream from the freezer after the 2 hours. Whisk and fold in the

crushed praline. Return to the freezer until firm. Scoop out small balls onto the foil-lined baking tray and open-freeze for about 4 hours, until hard.

Supporting each ice cream ball on the rounded end of a skewer or with the tips of 2 forks, dip quickly into the melted and cooled chocolate and return to the baking tray. Open-freeze for 30 minutes. Serve straight from the freezer chocolate sauce.

Serves 4–6

dulce de leche panna cotta

see variations page 281

The creaminess of this dessert is enhanced by the addition of dulche de leche. The combination is just heavenly.

3 tsp unflavoured gelatin
3–4 tbsp cold water
240 ml (8 fl. oz) full-fat milk
300 ml (10 fl. oz) thick cream

1 vanilla pod, split lengthwise and seeds
    scraped out
60 g (2 oz) sugar
1 370-g (13-oz) tin dulce de leche

In a small bowl, soak the gelatin in the water until soft.

In a medium pan, heat together the milk, cream, vanilla pod and seeds and sugar. Bring to a simmer, remove and discard the vanilla pod. Add the gelatin, remove the tin from the heat and stir until the gelatin has dissolved. Divide the mixture between 4 ramekins and allow to cool. Chill in the refrigerator until set, at least an hour.

To serve, turn each panna cotta out onto individual serving dishes and spoon out 1 or 2 spoonfuls of the dulce de leche from the can, keeping it nicely formed.

Serves 4

chocolate pecan brownies

see variations page 282

Everyone loves brownies and if you serve them warm, with ice cream, whipped cream and lots of chocolate and butterscotch sauces (pages 22 and 254), they are a really indulgent treat.

140 g (5 oz) dark chocolate,
   broken into pieces
170 g (6 oz) unsalted butter
4 eggs
170 g (6 oz) brown sugar
60 g (2 oz) rice flour
60 g (2 oz) ground almonds

60 g (2 oz) plain chocolate
   chips
40 g (1½ oz)
   chopped pecans
icing sugar,
   for dusting

ice cream, whipped cream,
   chocolate sauce and
   butterscotch sauce,
   to serve

Grease a 20x20-cm (8x8-in) square baking tin and preheat the oven to 175°C (350°F/Gas mark 4). In a medium saucepan, over a gentle heat, melt the bitter chocolate and butter together. Set aside to cool.

In a medium bowl, whisk the eggs and brown sugar until light and frothy, about 3 minutes. Stir in the melted and cooled chocolate and butter mixture. Fold in the rice flour, ground almonds, chocolate chips and pecans. Transfer to the baking tin and bake for about 30 minutes or until well risen and firm to the touch. Allow to cool in the tin, then cut into 9 squares and dust with icing sugar. To serve, place a brownie on a serving dish, add a spoonful of ice cream on top, followed by whipped cream and drizzles of chocolate and butterscotch sauces.

Serves 9

white chocolate & walnut maple blondies

see variations page 283

They say that true chocoholics love white chocolate more than any other and combining it with maple syrup and vanilla makes these simply divine.

110 g (4 oz) white rice flour
40 g (1½ oz) cornflour
50 g (1¾ oz) cornmeal
1 tsp baking powder
½ tsp xantham gum
½ tsp salt

110 g (4 oz) unsalted
    butter, softened, plus
    extra for greasing
140 g (5 oz) dark
    brown sugar
1 large egg, lightly beaten

120 ml (4 fl. oz) maple syrup
1 tsp vanilla extract
90 g (3 oz) chopped walnuts
60 g (2 oz) chopped
    white chocolate

Grease a 20x20-cm (8x8-in) baking tin and preheat the oven to 175°C (350°F/Gas mark 4).

In a medium bowl, whisk together the rice flour, cornflour, cornmeal, baking powder, xantham gum and salt until well blended. In another bowl, using an electric mixer, cream the butter with the dark brown sugar. Beat in the egg, add the flour mixture, maple syrup and vanilla. Continue to whisk until the batter is light and fluffy. Stir in the walnuts and white chocolate and transfer to the baking tin, smoothing the top with a palette knife. Bake for 25–30 minutes until slightly risen and golden brown.

Remove from the oven and cut into 9 squares. Leave in the tin to cool for 10 minutes, then lift out the slices onto a wire rack to cool completely.

Makes 9 blondies

variations

orange & polenta cake

see base recipe page 237

lemon drizzle cake

Prepare the basic recipe, omitting the oranges and substituting the zest of 3 lemons and the juice of 2. Use the juice from the third lemon to make a lemon drizzle by mixing it with 4 tablespoons sugar. While the cake is hot and still in the tin, make a few holes in the top with a cocktail stick and pour on the drizzle, allowing it to sink into the cake.

orange & polenta cake with pineapple

Prepare the basic recipe, adding 60 g (2 oz) drained crushed pineapple to the mixture with the orange zest and juice.

orange & polenta cake with orange glaze

Prepare the basic recipe. Sift 140 g (5 oz) icing sugar into a medium bowl and add 120 ml (4 fl. oz) freshly squeezed orange juice. Mix to form a thick glaze (which will not run off the cake) and smooth it over the cooled top.

dairy-free orange & polenta cake with golden raisins

Prepare the basic recipe, replacing the butter with dairy-free margarine and adding 85 g (3 oz) golden raisins with the orange zest and juice.

hazelnut meringue cake with raspberry coulis

see base recipe page 238

hazelnut meringue cake with chocolate sauce
Prepare the basic recipe, omitting raspberries and coulis. Gently heat
1 170-g (6-oz) tin evaporated milk with 60 g (2 oz) plain chocolate, stirring
continuously. Add 85 g (3 oz) brown sugar, simmer for 3 minutes. Serve with the
meringue.

hazelnut meringue cake with strawberries & raspberry coulis
Use sliced strawberries in the filling. Serve with raspberry coulis.

chocolate pavlova with fresh fruits
Instead of the basic recipe, make a meringue with 6 egg whites, ½ teaspoon white
wine vinegar, 2 tablespoons sifted Dutch process cocoa powder, 1 tablespoon
cornflour and 340 g (12 oz) sugar. Place a 9-in parchment paper circle on a baking
tray and spoon on the meringue, building up sides slightly. Bake at 135°F (275°F/
Gas mark 1) for 1½ hours. Cool. Pile whipped cream in the centre and decorate
with fresh fruit.

eton mess with raspberry coulis
Make the meringue, omitting the hazelnuts. Cool. Break into rough pieces and mix
with the whipped cream. Fold in 230 g (8 oz) hulled and sliced strawberries. Serve
in individual dishes, drizzled with raspberry coulis.

variations

carrot & pineapple cake with cream cheese frosting

see base recipe page 240

carrot & coconut cake with cream cheese frosting
Prepare the basic recipe, adding 60 g (2 oz) unsweetened shredded coconut to the batter with the carrots.

carrot & walnut cake with cream cheese frosting
Prepare the basic recipe, replacing the pecans with walnuts.

carrot & pineapple cake with golden raisins
Prepare the basic recipe, adding 85 g (3 oz) golden raisins to the batter with the carrots.

dairy-free carrot & pineapple cake
Prepare the basic recipe, omitting the frosting. Make a creamy frosting by beating together 170 g (6 oz) sifted icing sugar with 70 g (2½ oz) dairy-free margarine and 1 teaspoon vanilla extract until light and fluffy.

blueberry & lemon sponge dessert

see base recipe page 242

raspberry & coconut sponge dessert
Prepare the basic recipe, omitting the lemon zest and using 40 g (1½ oz) sweetened shredded coconut. Replace the blueberries with raspberries.

cherry sponge dessert
Prepare the basic recipe, omitting the lemon zest and replacing the blueberries with 110 g (4 oz) pitted cherries. Serve with a warmed 400-g (14-oz.) tin cherry pie filling as a sauce.

blueberry & lemon sponge dessert with cream cheese topping
Prepare the basic recipe. Make a topping by mixing 110 g (4 oz) sifted icing sugar with 1 230-g (8-oz) tub of cream cheese. Spread over the top of the cooled cake.

chocolate & pear sponge dessert
Prepare the basic recipe, omitting the lemon zest and using 85 g (3 oz) plain chocolate chips. Replace the blueberries with 2 or 3 peeled, cored and chopped pears.

dairy-free blueberry & lime sponge dessert
Prepare the basic recipe, replacing the butter with dairy-free margarine and the milk with rice milk. Replace 2 of the lemons with limes.

variations

chocolate & cherry roulade

see base recipe page 245

chocolate & cherry roulade with chocolate cream filling
Prepare the basic recipe. Add 85 g (3 oz) dark chocolate, melted and cooled, to the filling.

chocolate & raspberry roulade with brandy cream
Prepare the basic recipe, replacing the cherries with raspberries. Add 2 tablespoons brandy to the filling.

chocolate pecan roulade with coffee cream filling
Prepare the basic recipe, omitting the cherries and substituting 85 g (3 oz) chopped pecans. Add 2 teaspoons coffee extract to the filling.

dairy-free chocolate & cherry roulade with chocolate sauce
Prepare the basic roulade. Instead of the cream filling, beat 85 g (3 oz) dairy-free margarine with 2 teaspoons vanilla extract and 170 g (6 oz) sifted icing sugar until smooth. Spread onto roulade and add the cherries. Omit the decoration. Heat 170 g (6 oz) bitter chocolate, broken into pieces, with 150 ml (5 fl. oz) water, 1 teaspoon instant coffee powder and 60 g (2 oz) sugar. Simmer for 10 minutes and serve as a hot or cold sauce.

variations

strawberry jam roly-poly

see base recipe page 246

raspberry & lemon jam roly-poly
Prepare the basic recipe, replacing the strawberry jam with raspberry jam.
After spreading with the jam, add 1 tablespoon lemon curd to the centre of the
dough. Roll up as before.

strawberry & coconut roly-poly
Prepare the basic recipe, spreading 40 g (1½ oz) sweetened shredded coconut
on top of the jam.

strawberry jam roly-poly with custard
Prepare the basic recipe and serve it with custard. Heat 300 ml (10 fl. oz) full-
fat milk with 1 teaspoon vanilla extract, allowing it to just come to a boil. In a
medium bowl, beat 2 egg yolks with 1 tablespoon sugar, pour in the milk and
whisk vigorously. Return to tin and stir over low heat until the mixture
thickens, 5–6 minutes. Serve hot, warm or cold.

dairy-free lemon roly-poly
Prepare the basic recipe, replacing the butter with solid vegetable shortening.
Replace the strawberry jam with lemon curd. You can also serve this with
homemade dairy-free custard by substituting rice or oat milk for the full-fat
milk in the variation above.

strawberry shortcake cheesecake

see base recipe page 249

strawberry shortcake & white chocolate cheesecake
Add 170 g (6 oz) white chocolate chips to mixture before transferring to the tin.

chocolate chip & peanut butter cheesecake
Omit the sliced almonds from the basic recipe. Add 170 g (6 oz) chocolate chips and 85 g (3 oz) peanut butter chips to the mixture before transferring to the tin. Omit the strawberries and glaze from the topping.

raspberry shortcake cheesecake
Use raspberries in place of strawberries in the topping and glaze. Drop 60 g (2 oz) raspberries into the cheesecake before baking.

white chocolate & macadamia nut blondie cheesecake
Prepare the basic recipe, using the blondie recipe (page 267) in place of the shortcake. Swirl chopped macadamia nuts and caramel ice cream through the cheesecake before baking. Omit the topping and serve with whipped cream and caramel sauce.

cherry & almond cheesecake
Replace strawberries and jam in topping with 230 g (8 oz) cherry pie filling.

variations

french apple flan

see base recipe page 250

mixed berry flan with fromage frais
Instead of the basic recipe, bake the crust completely. Mix 450 g (1 lb) fromage frais with 6 tablespoons icing sugar and 2 teaspoons vanilla extract, spoon into crust, add assorted berries and drizzle with raspberry coulis (page 238).

sweet almond & coconut flan
Instead of the basic recipe, spread the part-baked crust with 4 tablespoons strawberry jam. Heat together 110 g (4 oz) each of butter and sugar, 60 g (2 oz) ground almonds and 40 g (1½ oz) shredded coconut. Spread evenly over jam and bake for 30–35 minutes at 190°C (375°F/Gas mark 5). Eat hot, warm or cold.

pecan pie
Instead of the basic recipe, whisk together 3 eggs, 140 g (5 oz) sugar, 230 g (8 oz) dark golden syrup and 70 g (2½ oz) melted butter. Add 170 g (6 oz) pecan halves, pour into an unbaked deep crust and bake for about 50 minutes at 175°C (350°F/Gas mark 4) until set. Allow to cool before serving.

dairy-free french apple flan
Prepare basic recipe, replacing dairy-free margarine with butter in the filling.

variations

sweet potato pie with toffee pecan sauce

see base recipe page 252

sweet potato & peanut butter pie with toffee pecan sauce
Prepare the basic recipe, omitting the orange zest, pumpkin pie spice, and brandy. Replace with 110 g (4 oz) smooth peanut butter and 60 g (2 oz) peanut butter chips.

sweet potato & butterscotch tart with toffee almond sauce
Prepare the basic recipe, omitting the orange zest, pumpkin pie spice and brandy. Replace with 170 g (6 oz) butterscotch chips. Replace the pecans in the sauce with sliced almonds.

sweet potato & almond pie with toffee almond sauce
Prepare the basic recipe, replacing the orange zest and pumpkin pie spice with 60 g (2 oz) ground almonds and 1 teaspoon almond extract. Replace the pecans in the sauce with sliced almonds.

sweet potato & apple pie with toffee pecan sauce
Prepare the basic recipe, adding 1 peeled, cored and chopped apple (such as a Golden Delicious) to the sweet potato purée.

variations

profiteroles with chocolate sauce

see base recipe page 254

profiteroles with lemon filling & lemon sauce
Prepare the basic recipe, adding 2 teaspoons lemon zest to the whipped cream filling. Omit the chocolate sauce and warm a jar of lemon curd for the sauce.

profiteroles with coffee-flavoured filling & chocolate sauce
Prepare the basic recipe, adding 2 teaspoons coffee extract to the whipped cream filling.

coffee choux pastries with icing
Prepare the basic recipe. Pipe circles of choux pastry to make small balls. Slice in half horizontally and fill with whipped cream. Make glacé icing by mixing together 230 g (8 oz) sifted icing sugar with a little water, 1 teaspoon coffee extract and 1 teaspoon glycerine. Spread across the top of the pastries with a knife.

chocolate eclairs with chocolate icing
Prepare recipe for coffee choux pastries (above), piping fingers of pastry to form eclairs. For the icing, substitute 60 g (2 oz) melted and cooled chocolate for the coffee extract.

variations

lemon mousse

see base recipe page 256

raspberry mouse
Replace the lemon juice with 6 tablespoons raspberry coulis (page 238). Add 110 g (4 oz) fresh raspberries with whisked egg whites.

passion fruit mousse
Omit the lemons from the basic recipe. Substitute the flesh and juice of 6 passion fruits, added with the whisked egg whites.

lemon & lime mousse
Prepare the basic recipe, substituting 1 lime for 1 lemon.

apricot mousse
Omit 2 lemons. Gently stew 450 g (1 lb) fresh apricots with 1 tablespoon water until tender. Remove from heat, discard stones and allow to cool. Add with the whisked egg whites.

dairy-free chocolate mousse
Instead of the basic recipe, slowly melt 170 g (6 oz) bitter chocolate with 1 tablespoon dairy-free margarine over a bain marie. Beat in 3 egg yolks and 1 tablespoon coffee extract, then fold in 3 stiffly beaten egg whites.

marsala poached peaches & mascarpone cream

see base recipe page 258

marsala poached nectarines & mascarpone cream
Prepare the basic recipe, substituting nectarines for the peaches.

marsala poached peaches with raspberry parfait
Prepare the basic recipe. Omit mascarpone cream. Freeze raspberry coulis
(page 238) for 2 hours. Whisk 2 egg whites until stiff, then whisk in 110 g
(4 oz) sugar until very stiff. Beat half-frozen coulis with a fork and add to
300 g (10 oz) whipped cream with the egg whites. Serve immediately in
chilled glasses with the peaches.

marsala poached peaches with fruit compote & mascarpone cream
Prepare the basic recipe. In a medium saucepan, heat together 230 g (8 oz)
sliced strawberries, 230 g (8 oz) raspberries, 110 g (4 oz) blackberries,
2 peeled and sliced apples and 450 g (1 lb) sugar. Simmer until soft,
and serve warm or cold with the mascarpone cream.

marsala poached peaches with brandy & oat cream
Prepare the basic recipe. Omit the mascarpone cream. Mix 2 tablespoons
toasted chopped almonds and 2 tablespoons toasted rolled oats into
300 g (10 oz) whipped cream with 1 tablespoon lemon juice, 4 tablespoons
honey and 4 tablespoons whiskey.

chocolate-covered praline ice cream balls

see base recipe page 260

chocolate chip ice cream with chocolate sauce
Prepare the basic recipe, omitting praline. Fold 170 g (6 oz) plain chocolate chips into the ice cream. Omit the chocolate covering and serve with chocolate sauce.

strawberry ice cream
Prepare the basic recipe, omitting praline. Fold 110 g (4 oz) chopped strawberries into the ice cream. Top with chopped strawberries and cream.

mint chocolate chip & chocolate-covered ice cream balls
Prepare the basic recipe, omitting praline. Fold 170 g (6 oz) plain chocolate chips and 2 teaspoons peppermint extract into the ice cream.

chocolate-covered milk chocolate & peanut butter ice cream balls
Prepare the basic recipe, omitting praline. Instead, fold 170 g (6 oz) mixed milk chocolate and peanut butter chips into the ice cream.

piña colada ice cream balls
Prepare the basic recipe, omitting praline. Instead, fold 40 g (1½ oz) sweetened shredded coconut, 40 g (1½ oz) drained crushed pineapple and 1 teaspoon coconut extract into the ice cream. Omit chocolate sauce.

dulce de leche panna cotta

see base recipe page 262

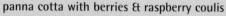

panna cotta with berries & raspberry coulis
Prepare the basic recipe. Omit the dulce de leche and serve with fresh mixed berries drizzled with raspberry coulis (page 238).

panna cotta with poached pears & chocolate sauce
Prepare the basic recipe. Omit dulce de leche and serve with 1 peeled, cored and halved pear per person, poached in red wine with mulled wine spices and 230 g (8 oz) sugar. Serve with chocolate sauce (page 254).

coffee panna cotta with whipped cream & maple syrup
Prepare the basic recipe, omitting the dulce de leche and adding 2 teaspoons instant coffee powder to the milk while it is heating. Serve with whipped cream and a drizzle of maple syrup.

white chocolate panna cotta with dulce de leche
Prepare the basic recipe, adding 170 g (6 oz) white chocolate morsels to the milk and cream mixture while it is heating,

dairy-free coconut panna cotta with strawberries
Replace the milk and cream with tinned coconut milk. Serve with sliced fresh strawberries and raspberry coulis (page 238).

variations

chocolate pecan brownies

see base recipe page 265

chocolate pecan brownies with white chocolate chips
Add 60 g (2 oz) white chocolate morsels with the nuts in the basic recipe.

chocolate mixed nut brownies
Add an extra 85 g (3 oz) chopped mixed nuts to the basic recipe, such as walnuts, almonds, Brazil and macadamia nuts.

chocolate brownies with chocolate cheesecake frosting
Omit the pecans and the toppings. Spread the well-cooled brownies with a mixture of 170 g (6 oz) cream cheese, 70 g (2½ oz) butter, 200 g (7 oz) sifted icing sugar and 30 g (1 oz) Dutch process cocoa powder.

chocolate brownies with caramel sauce
Prepare the basic recipe. Simmer together 85 g (3 oz) brown sugar, 140 g (5 oz) dark golden syrup, 60 g (2 oz) butter and 120 ml (4 fl. oz) thick cream 5 minutes. Remove from heat. Add 2 tablespoons lemon juice.

dairy-free chocolate pecan brownies with chocolate sauce
Prepare the basic recipe, replacing the butter with dairy-free margarine. Omit the topping and serve with dairy-free chocolate sauce (page 272).

white chocolate & walnut maple blondies

see base recipe page 267

white chocolate & macadamia maple blondies
Prepare the basic recipe, replacing the walnuts with chopped
macadamia nuts.

white chocolate & date maple blondies
Prepare the basic recipe, replacing the walnuts with 140 g (5 oz) chopped
dried dates.

butterscotch & pecan maple blondies
Prepare the basic recipe, replacing the white chocolate with butterscotch
chips and the walnuts with chopped pecans.

white chocolate & cherry maple blondies
Prepare the basic recipe, replacing the walnuts with dried cherries.

dairy-free peanut butter & walnut maple blondies
Prepare the basic recipe, replacing the white chocolate with dairy-free
peanut butter chips and the butter with dairy-free margarine.

index